THE PEOPLE'S CHOICE

William Burlie Brown

THE

The Presidential Image

PEOPLE'S

in the Campaign Biography

CHOICE

LOUISIANA STATE UNIVERSITY PRESS
BATON ROUGE · LOUISIANA

To

ROSEL GEORGE BROWN

who shared the labor and the fun

ACKNOWLEDGMENTS

THE AUTHOR GRATEFULLY ACKNOWLEDGES THE ASSISTANCE of Wendell H. Stephenson of the University of Oregon; Fletcher M. Green, Frank A. Klingberg, and J. Carlyle Sitterson of the University of North Carolina; William R. Hogan, Joseph P. Roppolo, and Charles Till Davis of Tulane University; and Thomas P. Govan, Executive Chairman for Faculty Work, National Council, Protestant Episcopal Church.

CONTENTS

LIST OF ILLUSTRATIONS

INTRODUCTION

ONCE EVERY FOUR YEARS THE PEOPLE OF THE UNITED STATES select their chief magistrate. This is a very serious business, for over the years since 1789 the office of President of the United States has grown to tremendous importance. The last fifty years have witnessed a great widening of the area under administrative control, until the hand of the executive can be discerned in almost every aspect of the nation's domestic affairs. Furthermore, in recent years foreign nations have sometimes felt it necessary to hold decisions on their own domestic affairs in abeyance until Americans have chosen their President. Yet a certain circus atmosphere surrounds the process by which Americans arrive at this awesome choice. For months preceding election day town and countryside are disfigured with posters, billboards, and street banners; the citizenry sport buttons, badges, and ribbons; they chant campaign slogans and sing campaign songs; they march for, talk for, and often fight for, the candidate of their choice.

How they determine their choice from among the candidates offered for their consideration is a problem of acute and continuing interest to both the academic student of American politics and the American politician—neither has as yet discovered the answer. While there are almost as many theories as there are students, in general these scholars agree that it is a complex problem. Part of this complexity, some contend, is due to an element of "irrationality" that enters into the voter's choice. This element of irrationality is an inference, deducible from the statistically verifiable fact that the voter does not always vote in accordance with his social and economic interests.

While this book is only tangentially concerned with the political behavior of the American people, it does address itself to the task of exploring some aspects of this alleged irrationality. Briefly, it offers an explanation which, while clearly not solving the riddle of the people's choice, may make some of the elements involved in that choice seem a bit more rational.

If this effect is achieved, it is because this book adopts a somewhat unusual approach to a presidential election. It views the choice of a President not from the point of view of a clash of powerful political personalities, or of economic interests, or from the standpoint of what are usually referred to as "the issues," but as a search for a symbol—a symbol that will represent the whole complex of ideals and beliefs that the American people have held dear. For the presidency has come to be, as one student of the political scene has acutely observed, "something more than an office based on law." It is "an institution whose character is deeply rooted in the American mood and culture. . . . a kind of cultural apotheosis in which the nation can see an image of its best aims. . . . the symbol of what Americans as a whole think or wish themselves to be." In Great Britain the Crown fills this need. Having abjured monarchy, it was inevitable that the people of the United States should fasten the task of symbolizing the nation upon the President. He is the one important official elected by all of the people. Neither remote and specialized like the Supreme Court nor large and diffuse like the Congress, the presidency, which concentrates powers and responsibilities in the person of one man, is the only constitutional branch of the national government that could conceivably serve as an adequate symbol.

It is the object of this book to explore the nature of this symbol. In the ensuing pages it will become clearly apparent that those who have labored for the election of presidential candidates ever since the days of Andrew Jackson have, with varying degrees of consciousness, been aware of the symbolic nature of the presidency. In every campaign since 1824 they have striven mightily to persuade the voter, through every medium of mass communication, that their candidate came closest to being what "Americans as a whole think or wish themselves to be." They have built this image in song and slogan and dinned it into the electorate in noisy torchlight processions. They have woven the fabric of this symbol with threads of golden oratory from the stump. They have inundated the body politic in oceans of print, fashioning this ideal man in posters, broadsides, newspapers, magazines, and books.

It is painfully apparent that a complete exploration of the nature of this symbol, involving as it must an examination of all of the media in which it is expressed, would be an impossible undertaking. Forced to choose from this bewildering mountain of material, the author selected what seemed to him the vehicle of propaganda that would enable him to come closest to an analysis of the symbol—the campaign biography.

Less boisterous than the songs, less spectacular than the banners and torchlights, less stirring than the oratory and the slogans, the campaign biography endures, gathering dust on library shelves. But of equal importance with its less ephemeral nature is the fact that it provides the most extensive amount of information about the candidate that is furnished to the voter in a single package during the campaign. It is, moreover, directed toward a national audience and is often the source for much of the material that appears in newspapers, magazines, and other campaign literature.

The campaign biography has been a consistent feature of every campaign since 1824. These biographies are neither scholarly productions nor pure fabrications. They are what an advertising-conscious civilization calls "promotional literature," designed to "sell the customer" a presidential candidate.

It is impossible to read more than a half dozen of these adroit pieces of political propaganda without becoming aware of the almost stereotyped method of appeal they employ. They are engaged in the creation of a symbol—a symbol compounded of a large number of the ideas, beliefs, images, ideals, and emotions that the American public reveres. This symbol they clothe with the flesh and animate with the words and actions of their subject. In short, they create out of the raw material of the candidate's real life the biography of an ideal citizen of the Republic. This has been the basic purpose of an unbroken succession of campaign biographies from John Quincy Adams to Richard Nixon. It is reasonable to conclude, therefore, that to regard a presidential election as the choice of a symbol by the electorate is to adopt a viewpoint sanctioned by the practice of generations of politicians.

The political effectiveness of the campaign biography is about as measurable as the effect of "rain in the upstate counties." Nevertheless, it need only be indicated that presidential campaign managers and their associates are notoriously pragmatic in their approach to campaigning, and no campaign since 1824 has failed to produce at least one campaign biography. Since the exclusive concern here is the biographies themselves and the symbol they have created, it is not necessary to go beyond this logical inference of their effectiveness.

In the creation of this symbol, this ideal citizen of the republic, the campaign biographer has furnished the historians of the American mind a very relevant bit of material. Charged with the mission of selling the candidate to the voter, he appeals, like his "ad man" counterpart, to ideals and images that he feels sure the voter reveres. Since he is engaged in narrating the events of a life that has usually covered fifty or more years, he has to marshal a host of these surefire appeals. He must identify the candidate with ideas the public holds about ancestry and good parents, evoke an image of the ideal child and youth, and compound the complex of ideas that go into the making of an ideal soldier, professional man, and statesman. Thus the finished product represents not only the ideal citizen but also, for the student of American culture, at least a partial catalogue of American ideals and beliefs.

THE PEOPLE'S CHOICE

1————

HERALDS OF DESTINY
On the Making of Campaign Biographies

For 136 years an unbroken procession of campaign lives has been given to the public—all dedicated to the same purpose, all following almost identical methods, all building essentially the same image; all, in short, bearing a striking resemblance. Surely, it would seem reasonable to assume that there must be some well-oiled mechanism for their steady and faithful production. But this is emphatically not the case. The search to discover how campaign lives come to be written has not been futile, however. Instead, it has led to many answers, too many to permit sound generalization. Ultimately, it is necessary to conclude that while the question can be answered for each individual campaign biography, no categorical answer can be found for the origin of campaign biographies generally.

When the focus is shifted from the campaign lives themselves to the broader area of American presidential politics in which they are designed to function, this discovery ceases to seem startling. Indeed, given the nature of our national party politics, it is difficult to see how any other answer could be possible. The simple truth is that no "well-oiled mechanism" has ever existed. The late Alfred E. Smith remarked to a reporter after his defeat in November of 1928 that "it has been the habit of the Democratic party to function only six months in every four years." This was an exaggeration, of course, spiced with a small bunch of sour grapes, but it serves to point up the solid fact that each of the two great national parties is, in essence, a rather loose confederation of local political groups that seldom exhibit pronounced symptoms of national organization except during presidential elections.

The Democratic party has had a national committee since 1848; the Republican party started off with one for its first presidential

3

campaign in 1856. But to cast the national committee in the role of a board of directors of a vast organization, maintaining an imposing headquarters served by a huge staff of experts of long experience who have accumulated over the years a tremendous file of useful information and records, is about as mistaken a notion as one can entertain. The committee's chief, if not only, function lies in the political work that its individual members perform in their own state. Indeed, the committee usually assembles only three times in its four-year term.

The national chairman, for all practical purposes, *is* the national organization. Moreover, he has been, customarily, neither the committee's choice nor the party's, but the choice of the party's presidential nominee. Since 1856 the Republican party has had thirty-five national chairmen. Even in the long history of the Democratic party there have been relatively few men who have held the chairmanship for any considerable period of time. When a new chairman takes over he will generally bring with him his lieutenants, and often a new staff will be recruited almost from the office boy up. There is, in short, no discernible continuity.

While it is true that millions of dollars are spent by both major parties and that the national committee through its chairman is the dispenser of these funds, the major portion of the money is raised and spent in the presidential year. The staff may run into the hundreds and the office space rented into the acres, but for a few months only. The lean years invariably set in, whether political victory is achieved or not, for it would indeed be a rare phenomenon for a national chairman to finish a presidential campaign with money left over. As the chairman devotes himself to the task of trying to pay the bills that arrive after November 15, along with the messages of congratulation or condolence, retrenchment is reflected in the drastically diminished size of the staff and the very modest lodgings of the headquarters.

As for those vast files representing decades of political know-how, they simply do not exist. Correspondence is destroyed after six months or a year. Printed material is apparently thrown away in great quantity; both Republican and Democratic national committees retain only a small fraction of the books, pamphlets, and periodicals which they have issued or authorized. Their apology for what the historian must regard as utterly barbarous house-

4

keeping habits can, it is believed, be accepted as valid, what with the small size of their staffs and their crowded quarters.

When all of these factors are considered it is obvious that presidential campaigns are not mass-produced stereotypes ground from the mill by experienced assembly-line workers. They are, rather, the individual product of one or more men who bring to the task a wide variety of political experience. This is not to say that "tried and true" political techniques are not repeated over and over again, but, rather, that there is no machinery permanently set up to insure that they will be used. If a national chairman follows the methods of his predecessor, it is because his political wisdom, or lack of it, leads him to do so. Expediency is the guide.

Viewed thus in context, it is not at all surprising that there are no categorical answers to the questions: How and by whom are campaign biographers selected? Who pays for the publication? How are they distributed? These questions can be answered for individual campaign biographies, and a brief glance at some of these answers will furnish a fair idea of the wide diversity of their origin.

Some candidates, in a sense, prepared their own campaign biographies. The most famed of these are the two autobiographical sketches prepared by Lincoln which served as a basis for the many 1860 biographies. Horace Greeley's autobiography, although written earlier, was reprinted for the campaign of 1872. While never a candidate, John C. Calhoun was perennially hopeful, and historians have long accused him of writing his own campaign biography.

Sometimes the biographer is asked to perform this service by the candidate himself. At the outset of the campaign of 1876 Rutherford B. Hayes wrote to William Dean Howells (who had apparently opened the subject): "It would particularly please me to be honored by your doing it. No doubt your work would sell." Nathaniel Hawthorne had had a similar experience. Despite his later protestations to friends that he was put upon out of friendship to Franklin Pierce, Hawthorne wrote to Pierce on the day after his nomination, offering to undertake the campaign life. Pierce immediately took him up on it. Benjamin Harrison selected his friend and Civil War comrade-in-arms, General Lew Wallace, as his biographer in 1880. George F. Parker later wrote concerning his biography of Grover Cleveland for the 1892 campaign: "It drew materials and inspiration from its subject, had been prepared at his request, and was published with his co-operation and over-sight." Both Wendell Willkie and Thomas E. Dewey chose Stanley T. Walker to write their biographies.

Often the task has been taken up by one of the guiding spirits of the campaign. John Henry Eaton, later to acquire more endur-ing fame as the husband of the notorious Peggy than as Secretary of War, prepared a new edition of his biography of Jackson for the 1824 campaign. John Bigelow, then part owner and editor with William Cullen Bryant of the New York *Evening Post,* began his campaign life of John C. Frémont shortly after convincing the Pathfinder that he should become a candidate. Elihu B. Washburne, personal friend of Lincoln and later the sole person to greet him on his secret arrival in Washington on the eve of the inauguration, produced a campaign life of his fellow Illinoisian for the campaign that he did much to win in 1860. John W. Forney, back in the Democratic fold after long years as a Republican editor and politi-cian, took on the task of biographer of Winfield Scott Hancock for the campaign of 1880. Franklin Roosevelt and Henry Moskowitz each wrote one of Al Smith. Moskowitz and his wife Belle were among Smith's top advisers. It was, of course, FDR's "Happy Warrior" speech in the 1928 convention that placed Smith in nomination.

In numerous other ways the parties have contributed to the birth of campaign biographies. The range of party participation, from the selection of the biographer to the exercise of pressure on private publishing ventures, to the assumption of full publish-ing responsibilities, can all be illustrated from the 1860 cam-paign biographies of Lincoln alone. John Nicolay, Lincoln's secre-tary, believed that "some member of the Republican Committee" chose William Dean Howells, much to the chagrin of Nicolay, who was hoping to be asked to write Lincoln's campaign biography. (At least this is the story of John Nicolay's granddaughter. If Miss Nicolay is correct, then Lincoln must not have been aware of this selection, for the announcement by Howells' publishers that the biography was "Authorized by Mr. Lincoln" brought an angry denial from him. Howells' own explanation is that he was engaged by the publisher.) In at least two instances powerful pressure was brought to bear on publishing firms to change politi-

6

cally damaging material in the 1860 campaign lives of Lincoln, which these firms had undertaken as private ventures. There is reason to believe that still a third biography, by the radical abolitionist Ichabod Codding, was suppressed by Republican politicians. After all, it was a large part of the political attractiveness of their candidate that his closet was utterly innocent of abolitionist skeletons. Finally, the Republican committee actually published Elihu Washburne's campaign life.

Replying to inquiries from the author concerning the role of the two major parties in the publication of seven recent campaign biographies, publishers disclosed that one biography was subsidized; two were printed in a special paperbound edition for the party; three were neither subsidized before publication nor "adopted" afterward. In 1954 the incumbent chairmen of both the Republican and Democratic parties disclaimed any knowledge of campaign biographies being sponsored or paid for by the national committees.

Finally, a great many campaign biographies were launched as private publishing ventures by enterprising firms in the hope of capitalizing on the public interest in the campaign. The competition was very keen, and the race was to the swift. Often these biographies were ready for distribution within a few weeks after the nomination. As soon as the nomination was made, publishers began advertising extravagantly that they would have ready a biography within two or three weeks, or that it was "in press," and even that it was "now ready."

Some publishers gambled on the outcome of the convention in an effort to beat the rest of the trade. The most recent example of a successful guess is Noel F. Busch's *Adlai Stevenson*, which became a best seller. One publisher guessed wrong in 1860 and was stuck with a large stock of campaign lives of William H. Seward. Of course, many of these preconvention biographies are financed by those working for the nomination of a particular candidate. In 1954 Leonard W. Hall, chairman of the Republican National Committee, wrote that "It would be safe to assume that the hiring of the author and paying for his services would be taken care of by a committee of this kind." Although an examination of a number of these discloses that they are, as expected, no different from the postconvention variety, these preconvention

7

biographies have not been used here for two reasons: 1) their number is legion, and 2) they did not generally achieve a wide circulation. Where the preconvention biography was a correct guess, however, it is of course used.

To have their publication adopted by the party and given "official" or "authorized" status was a much-sought-after objective. Lincoln was plagued with publishers who "came to Springfield hoping to arrange for an 'authorized' life of the candidate." Benjamin Harrison had an exchange with the Judge Publishing Company, which wired him just a week after the nomination for "exclusive right to publish your authorized biography in book form." Yet many publishers must have met with more success than those who harassed Lincoln and Little Ben because a considerable number of campaign biographies bear the legend prominently displayed— "Authorized Edition."

Regardless of whether the campaign biography was written by a campaign manager, a party wheelhorse, a man selected by the candidate or by the candidate's manager, or by someone designated by a publishing house, and regardless of whether the publication was party inspired, adopted as official, or simply a private venture without party blessing, the candidate was very often consulted by the biographer, and he nearly always proved helpful. Occasionally a candidate collaborated closely with his biographer. Hayes wrote to his biographer, "No doubt a half barrell of stuff—letters, speeches, memoranda, diaries, etc. etc.—can be sent to you, out of which you would get up a romance that would be taking."

Frémont's biographer worked in close collaboration with Jesse Benton Frémont, the Pathfinder's highly literate wife. Sometimes, like Hayes and Ben Harrison, the candidate prepared a sketch of parts of his career not well known to the biographer. Publishers constantly urged, and with fair success, that the candidate or some representative designated by the candidate at least read and correct the proofs. Finally, the most frequent service rendered biographers by the candidates was submitting to be interviewed concerning the events of their personal history. Typical of this particular hardship in the life of a presidential candidate is the scene described with cloying cuteness by a biographer of James A. Garfield: "The general set himself down beside me and announced he was ready

8

to have his life taken. Then I got at him in true interviewer fashion and he submitted most gracefully."

Determining how campaign biographies originated is a far easier task than tracking down the answer to the problem of how they were put into the hands of the voter. One thing seems certain: they were not intended for mass distribution on the same scale as the less costly campaign literature (handbills, leaflets, and pamphlets) and the buttons, badges, and posters.

One early method of distribution was to call upon the postmasters to subscribe to a number of copies, which they would presumably peddle in their own bailiwicks. In the overall view, however, the preponderance of the evidence indicates that they were given away, but probably only to active campaigners, for the number of copies purchased by the parties seems small. Publishers report that in recent campaigns not more than 20,245 copies of a campaign life were sold to either party. (The possibility remains, of course, that interested individuals might buy and distribute campaign lives in quantity. This would be very difficult to establish since it could be done through book dealers without disclosing the purchasers.) Possibly much heavier purchases were made in earlier campaigns. Hawthorne consented to the free distribution of 5,000 copies of his campaign life of Pierce in New York City alone. Ben Wade, already an astute politician in 1852, mentions in a letter to his wife that the Whigs were "getting out about a million" copies of the life of Winfield Scott. James A. Farley gives a good account of the method of distribution employed in more recent times. Apparently, until he and Louis Howe came on the scene it was the practice of the Democratic party to ship sizable packages of assorted campaign literature to the various state campaign headquarters. They changed this to the more adroit method of sending small packages to individual local workers.

Probably a much larger number of campaign lives came into the hands of the voters through their own purchases. Figures on sales, especially for the nineteenth century, are both difficult to obtain and more than a little untrustworthy, but what is available indicates a fairly brisk sale. One Chicago bookseller boasted of a sale of 7,000 copies of campaign biographies of Frémont in 1856. It has been estimated that "certainly 100,000 and possibly

9

as many as 200,000 copies of Lincoln's biographies were distributed during the campaign of 1860." On the other hand, Howells wrote woefully to Mark Twain that "the Life of Hayes hasn't sold 2,000 copies." Publishers apparently *counted* on heavy sales, for they frequently furnished cheap editions and discounts for bulk purchase. Weeks, Jordan and Company of Boston, publishers of two campaign lives of William Henry Harrison in 1840, offered one of them at $1.80 per dozen, $13.50 per hundred, and $120.00 per thousand and the other at $6.00 per hundred, $48.00 per thousand, and $425 per ten thousand.

Yet with all this diversity of origin, sponsorship, and distribution, campaign biographies have a common purpose—to further the aspirations of the candidate. That they are designed as persuasive propaganda rather than objective biography is easily verifiable by the most casual sampling among the hundreds of them that have issued from the nation's presses since 1824.

Although many campaign biographers frankly admit the partisan purpose behind their work, an equally large number vigorously deny it. These denials range from the ingenuous rationalization to the blunt statement. Hawthorne's approach is a good example of the former. He insisted that his work could not possibly "operate upon the minds of multitudes, during a presidential canvass. [For] this species of writing is too remote from his customary occupations . . . to be satisfactorily done. . . ." In his biography of Al Smith, Roosevelt's simple disclaimer that "In no way is this written as a partisan plea" illustrates the latter approach. Many others, while neglecting to confirm or deny that they are writing a campaign biography, offer the loftiest sort of rationale for launching their books. This last group, which flourished especially throughout the nineteenth century when the "art of the preface" was in flower, runs the gamut of philosophical ideas on the value of biography.

Among these prefatory essays that set forth the *raison d'être* for the work the "gentle reader" is about to take up, two themes are encountered most frequently. The first of these is the ancient idea that the lives of great and good men serve as a lesson and inspiration; thus the biographer casts himself in the role of pedagogue. Typical of this approach is the explanation of the famous inspirational lecturer Russell H. Conwell of his object in writing the biography of James G. Blaine: "The young will profit by its examples of heroism, self-sacrifice, and perseverance; those in middle life will be encouraged and inspired by its record of well-earned success, after years of toil; and the old will find in it comfort and entertainment, as it accounts for their failure or explains their success."

The second theme discloses the biographer as a herald of destiny —the idea that the hour calls forth the man, and it is the function of the biographer to record how fate has prepared this man for this moment. The electorate has heeded some heralds like the biographer of Woodrow Wilson, who undertook to disclose "by what route . . . Fate decreed to land her man," and ignored others like the biographer who came to announce the advent of Dewey as "the perfect example of the right man at the right time." The mystic extent to which this can be carried is well illustrated by the following passage from a campaign life of Garfield: "At the moment Garfield was nominated a magnificent bald eagle, after arching round the park, swooped down and rested on the general's house."

Often the biographer varies this theme slightly; injecting a theistic note, he proclaims that the Lord has raised up a champion. Philosophizing on the elevation of Calvin Coolidge to the presidency after Warren Harding's death, his biographer points out the workings of Divine Providence. "The voice of the people seemed like a response in the words of an ancient chant:

> The stone which the builders rejected
> Is become the head of the corner.
> This is the Lord's doing;
> It is marvellous in our eyes."

Whether the biographer admits that his work is for the purpose of furthering the campaign of a presidential aspirant or assigns lofty motives for its preparation, he almost invariably asserts that his treatment is objective, is free of partisanship, and is based upon an honest and laborious collection of the facts of the candidate's life. It is, of course, impossible to take either the claims to objectivity or the protestations of high purpose with any degree of seriousness. Indeed, it is the identity of purpose easily discernible in all campaign biographies that gives them, despite their diversity of origin, a high degree of uniformity and permits generalizations

11

about them. United in their objective, they achieve their goal by a remarkable similarity in method.

This is true regardless of the literary capacity of the authors. An amazing variety of literary practitioners have produced campaign biographies, from distinguished authors like Hawthorne to hack writers of popular juvenile fiction like Oliver Optic and William Makepeace Thayer. Popular writers like Lew Wallace and Stanley Walker have turned them out. One of the most celebrated lecturers of the late nineteenth century, Russell Conwell, produced three. Renowned historians have written them: Richard Hildreth ground out one of William Henry Harrison in 1840, and George Bancroft wrote one of Martin Van Buren for the campaign of 1844. (Van Buren failed to receive the Democratic nomination and the biography was not published until 1889.) Journalists, for example Parson Brownlow, Henry J. Raymond, David Croly, and Noel F. Busch, have been the most numerous writers of campaign biographies. Yet there is little discernible difference in the level of sophistication in campaign lives regardless of who wrote them. The appeals, the language, and the presentation of the author of *The Scarlet Letter*, turned campaign biographer, cannot be distinguished from those employed by the author of the Boat Club Series, in his campaign life.

It is true that nearly all of these biographies were produced in great haste. The amount of time between the nomination and the election is not long, and it is important to bring one's persuasive techniques to bear upon the great electorate as soon as possible. The speed with which campaign biographers have turned out books which generally average three hundred pages is well-nigh incredible. Probably the record is held by Croly, who wrote, in one week, the campaign life of Horatio Seymour, Democratic hopeful in 1868. More typical is Howells' experience. Writing to a friend, he explained, "I am actually writing the Hayes book in three weeks— reading the immense mass of material, making copy, and correcting proof all at once. . . . I'm almost dead."

The fraternity of campaign biographers has constantly sent up a chorus of protest and apology for having to offer the reader a work so hastily executed. One encounters in almost every preface a disclaimer such as this: "It is but just to remark that circumstances have compelled us to prepare the volume with great haste,

12

so that the reader who is expecting a volume of elegant writing stands in a fair way to be disappointed. . . ." Yet while their cries of anguish over the tribulations of authorship under such conditions can be accepted as at least a partial explanation for the dead level of literary craftsmanship these biographies exhibit, they do not explain the consistency with which the same appeals, the same level of approach, and the same manner of presentation are used again and again.

Before undertaking a presentation and analysis of these appeals, which is the object of this book, it might be well to point out at this juncture that the campaign biographies do contain discussion of the issues of the canvass. Because of the emphasis here on appeals that have nothing to do with the issues, the false impression may be created that these campaign lives deliberately avoid mention of anything resembling a political issue. This is not intended. Indeed, it is the rare campaign biography that is completely silent on the candidate's views on current topics.

The amount of political discussion included in the biographies varies widely, but on the whole it usually occupies a lesser share of space than is devoted to the events of the candidate's life. The kind of political discussion included is much more homogeneous. Far and away, the most popular political issues that candidates take their stand upon are past issues, and they adopt the viewpoint that has proved to be favored. An outstanding illustration of this is the treatment of the slavery question in post-Civil War biographies. All candidates were reputed to have been strongly antislavery. As late as 1884 Blaine's campaign biographer was taking a strong stand on the slavery issue, proclaiming that his subject had hated slavery since childhood. Other than this sort of impregnable position, the stand taken on current issues is not more specific and unequivocating than the party platforms. For example, Coolidge's stand on the race problem in the midst of the Ku Klux Klan revival is "revealed" by his biographer thus: "He showed the white South that he could express to the negroes his convictions that they were justifying Lincoln's faith, without giving a rebuff to the new but characteristic impulse among the best Southern leaders toward fuller and fairer understanding between the races."

There is a discernible evolution over the years in the manner in which campaign biographers have presented this political discussion. Apparently the capacity of our ancestors for absorbing great "gobs" of political oratory in printed form was considerably greater than our own. The tendency of the earlier biographers was to sandwich huge slices of oratory into their narrative, particularly in the chapters that deal with the political career of the candidate. Gradually, the speeches, papers, and letters came to be relegated to the end of the narrative. There is, further, an increasing subtlety in the ability of biographers to demonstrate the candidate's stand on issues by anecdote and action rather than by spelling it out editorially or incorporating speeches and letters into the narrative.

Withal, it can be safely stated that the campaign biographies do not provide first-rate material for a study of campaign issues. But they do provide an excellent source for an examination of those appeals that were thought to strike the American voter much deeper than his temporary and changing opinions on political questions of the moment. In the following chapters, the most obvious and the most recurrent of these appeals will be presented. The objectives of this presentation are twofold: first, to set forth the appeals as they have been distilled by a close analysis of the campaign biographies and to note the changes that these appeals have undergone between 1824 and 1960; and second, to attempt to relate each appeal and its evolution to the society toward which it was directed.

PART ONE: Forebears

2———

THE BLOOD OF HEROES
The Ancestry of the Candidate

CAMPAIGN BIOGRAPHERS, ALMOST WITHOUT EXCEPTION, have recognized the existence of the ambivalent American attitude toward the importance of being well ancestored. They are well aware of the simultaneous tendencies toward pride in lineage (a trait that has made genealogy a big business and has given birth to numerous ancestor-worship societies) and toward the democratic insistence that a man is to be evaluated upon the basis of what he himself has achieved. Yet few have had the courage to confront the American public with this paradox as bluntly as did the biographer of General Ulysses S. Grant in 1868: "We profess here to despise blood and lineage; but no aristocracy is more inquisitive respecting the pedigree of its distinguished men." The general tendency is for the biographer to deny (often in sonorous indignation that such a denial should be necessary) that ancestors count for anything in "a government like ours [where] the faded pages of ancestral records weigh little against the living realities of the present." Indeed, this theme furnished the nineteenth-century biographers with a seldom-scorned opportunity to contrast our "republican institutions" with the "thralling prejudices of the old world." Having denounced "a fanatical veneration for blood as such," the biographer, with an air of condescension, adds "but for those that attach any weight to pedigree . . ." and proceeds to supply genealogical data, often in a fair amount of detail and not uncommonly running to eight or ten pages.

Up to the moment, no candidate has been able to match the phenomenal "Coolidge luck"—not only to have been born on the Fourth of July but also to have "in order that the President might be unmistakably American . . . a dash of Indian blood." Having to be content with being less American than Coolidge, the candidates nearly all lay claim to sturdy, tyranny-hating Old World ancestors who battled in the cause of religious or political liberty.

Usually their ancestry is British. If English, they may be descended from an old Cromwellian like the Harrisons, whose ancestor swapped "his butcher's apron for a martial cloak," rose to the rank of lieutenant-general, then attained the twin apotheosis of regicide judge and "martyr to the cause of constitutional liberty." Or, less spectacularly, their ancestor, like Hayes's, may have hidden a fugitive regicide, or have been simply "connected by marriage with Oliver Cromwell," like Samuel J. Tilden's family.

The romantic lore of Highland clans, perennially popular in nineteenth-century America, provided frequent opportunity for casting Scottish ancestors in heroic mold. Thus Blaine's ancestors could be numbered "among the brave adherents of the Scottish Prince Charlie," along with those of Winfield Scott. Hayes, in addition to his Cromwellian ancestors, his biographer asserted, could boast of an ancestry that went back to 1280 "when Hayes and Rutherford were two Scottish chieftains, fighting side by side with Baliol, William Wallace and Robert Bruce."

If the candidate's European forebears were French, they were, with rare exceptions, Huguenot. Thus the Garfields, the Hoovers (originally Huber), and the Deweys (originally Douai) fled the religious persecutions of the French monarchy and sought freedom of conscience in America, Holland, and England respectively.

In Germany, the tyranny-hating ancestors of Wendell Willkie fought Prussian autocracy and fled to America after the unsuccessful revolution of 1848. The Eisenhowers had preceded them, fleeing the Rhineland "during the Thirty Years War" in order "to avoid religious persecution."

An even more sharply defined pattern emerges in the biographers' treatment of their candidates' American forebears. Howells, in a mood of levity rare among campaign biographers, came very close to an exact statement of this pattern: "It is necessary that every American should have an indisputable grandfather, in order to be represented in the Revolutionary period by actual ancestral service, or connected with it by ancestral reminiscence. Further back than a grandfather few can go with satisfaction. Everything lies wrapt in colonial obscurity and confusion; and you have either to claim that the Smiths came over in the Mayflower, or that the Joneses were originally a Huguenot family of vast wealth and the gentlest blood, or that the Browns are descended from the race of Powhattan in the direct line; or you are left in an extremely embarrassing uncertainty as to the fact of great grandparents."

Seventeenth-century immigrants are the most desirable ancestors —the earlier in the century the better, of course. Thus it is passing strange that that nautical wonder of infinite capacity, the *Mayflower*, should have put out to sea with the ancestors of only two presidential candidates—Tilden and Franklin Roosevelt. The Garfields did, however, manage to book passage on the same boat with Governor John Winthrop.

Date and place of settlement lend an air of authenticity to claims of seventeenth-century forebears. It must have been a considerable source of satisfaction to his biographer to be able to write of Coolidge that "the original ancestors, John and Mary, established themselves in Watertown in 1630"; or to the biographer of Grover Cleveland, who could say that "Moses Cleveland emigrated from Ipswich, Suffolk County, England, in 1635." But lack of these confident details does not deter the biographer from placing his candidate's ancestors among the early bands of intrepid adventurers to the New World; it merely broadens his language. He claims, like the biographers of Zachary Taylor, that "the family of the Virginia Taylors is allied to the oldest . . . of that state," or like the biographer of Stephen A. Douglas, that the Douglas ancestors settled in Connecticut "during the early period of our colonial settlements."

Where it proved impossible to have the candidate's ancestors arrive in the seventeenth century, a valiant effort was made to establish them in the colonies in time for participation in the Revolution. The Jacksons managed to get in under the wire in 1765; the Blaines, arriving "about 1722–3," had a bit more time to get ready for the Redcoats.

The War of Independence furnishes endless opportunity for the discovery of heroic ancestors. These range from a signer of the Declaration, like the Harrisons' ancestor, to private soldiers. These were stirring times, indeed almost beyond the purview of mere prose.

Hawthorne's account of the glorious ancestor of Franklin Pierce

19

can be taken as a fairly representative example of how the campaign biographer, although denied the use of iambic pentameter, rose to the occasion: "On the 19th of April, 1775, being then less than eighteen years of age, the stripling was at the plough, when tidings reached him of the bloodshed at Lexington and Concord. He immediately loosened the ox chain, left the plough in the furrow, took his uncle's gun and equipments, and set forth towards the scene of action." This was in good Democrat tradition, for Jackson himself, that "intrepid and ardent boy, encouraged by his patriotic mother, hastened, at the age of fourteen, in company with one of his brothers, to the American camp, and enlisted in the service of his country." There were no Tories, no indifferents, no deserters or "sunshine patriots" in the background of any presidential candidate. Where no soldier is mentioned, there will be at least, as in the case of Van Buren's forebears, "a firm Whig."

Almost without exception the biographies that do not follow the pattern of seventeenth- (or early eighteenth-) century ancestors whose descendants served honorably, often heroically, in the Revolution maintain a discreet silence in the matter of ancestors.

This pattern shows very little variation from 1824 to the present. The amount and kind of attention given to ancestors is much the same throughout. Even though no candidate of southern or eastern European origin has yet appeared, it would seem reasonable to expect a change in the pattern with the coming of "the new immigration." But there is neither a diminution of emphasis upon ancestry nor any swing toward praise of the melting-pot process.

The one change that is noteworthy occurs in the twentieth century. Where the nineteenth-century biographers with one hand earnestly denounced what they considered an unrepublican tendency toward the veneration of distinguished ancestry and on the other catered to that tendency, the twentieth-century biographers seem oblivious or indifferent to the need for conforming to this ambivalent attitude in their readers. Superficially, their language seems closely parallel to their predecessors'; for example, one biographer of Wilson began her discussion of ancestry thus: "Sticklers who insist that a square inch of heredity germinates more character than a square mile of environment will be gratified to discover. . . ." But on a closer look it will appear that the damaging impact of the word "heredity" is gone and its meaning has been altered radically in the twentieth century. Gone, too, are the denials of its importance and the accompanying disquisition on the superiority of republican institutions over decadent European tradition. The twentieth-century biographers present the lineage of their subject without apology, in an offhand, sometimes bantering, manner. Stevenson, his biographer reports, "worships his ancestors like the Japanese."

The campaign biographer, in seeking to fashion the ideal American out of the raw material furnished by the life history of his subject, encounters at the very outset a delicate, perplexing, and paradoxical situation. The situation is not of his making; it is endemic to his country. Born of revolution, it has shuddered at the word. Trampling upon tradition, it has cherished the tattered remains. Asserting the rights of man, it has always loved a lord.

The factors that produced the American democratic ideal of assessing a man on the basis of his individual worth and denying that his ancestors have any bearing on the matter are easy to determine, for at least superficially they are logically deducible from the leading events of the nation's history. Thus they have come in for the lion's share of historical treatment. The heritage of the Revolution with the ringing pronouncements of the Declaration and the challenging phrases of *Common Sense;* the Jeffersonian rout of Federalist "aristocracy"; the evangelical democracy of the age of Jackson with its passionate faith in the mission of America to pull down every form of tyranny everywhere; the mystical democratizing influence of the Turnerian frontier—all have received lavish attention from the writers of our history.

It is the other half of the paradox that is difficult to probe. On the same level of superficiality it is illogical to expect a veneration of ancestors in a people who equated ancestry with heredity, heredity with aristocracy, and aristocracy with tyranny. Such pride in ancestry would seem out of place in a nation where a Virginia aristocrat felt obliged to apologize for recording his family history since "at this day it is deemed arrogant to remember one's ancestors." And a wealthy South Carolinian replied to Scottish traveler Alexander

Mackay's question about genealogy: "We don't vally [*sic:* value] these things in this country . . . it's what's above ground, not what's under, that we think on."

The desire to be well ancestored, to cling to tradition and to an aristocratic class organization has not gone unnoticed by historians. But most frequently it has been treated as a phenomenon that begins to wane by 1800 and, if not banished, is driven underground by the torrent of Jacksonian democracy that breaks over the land in the 1830's. Yet there is considerable evidence that this lingering aristocratic tendency in the mind of Americans freshly poured from the crucible of revolt is not a temporary thing which fades with the passage of time. It has permeated all areas of life, revealing itself in countless guises. True enough, a slow erosion aided by sporadic resurgence of the egalitarian spirit has had its effect. But this effect has been to change the outward badges rather than to kill the spirit of aristocratic pretension. After the American Revolution, college students were no longer openly listed by social rank but the colleges, privately, continued to maintain such a list. Social rank continued to determine the order of march of the citizens who took part in the public processions that marked the opening of terms of court.

Daniel Webster's prediction that General Jackson would "bring a breeze with him," was indeed borne out. But even ardent Jacksonians, who scented "aristocracy" in every wind, delighted in bestowing "republican titles" like "Judge" and "Captain" on local worthies. While this last ought not to be taken too seriously as an aristocratic pretension, there is evidence enough that the desire to be exalted above the ordinary level of common humanity by virtue of the "blood line" has persisted throughout the nation's history. Regardless of the degree of importance that should be attached to it, the flourishing growth of Society from the beginning of our history to the present, bringing with it the ubiquitous Society Page, the Blue Book, the Four Hundred, and the early establishment and persistence of innumerable ancestor-worship societies, are reflections of the aristocratic spirit.

The aristocratic principle has been a potent force in the history of mankind for so long that it would be absurd to suppose that it could be cast off in a few brief years. Indeed, its long persistence has led many with a flair for Olympian pronouncements on the

nature of man to suppose it a "natural" or "instinctive" characteristic of the race. Others, preferring the sweat of the arena to this
atmosphere of clinical detachment, have tended to divide mankind into two warring factions—the few and the many. Long and
loud has the controversy raged over the problem of whether the
American Revolution was a "gentleman's revolt" or a great democratic upheaval, over the degree to which Hamilton was a "mon-
archist," the degree to which Jefferson was a democrat, the degree
to which the Federalists were aristocratic, the Republicans democratic.

Possibly, as some have suggested, it is unnecessary to regard
the aristocratic principle as a natural characteristic of man or to
choose up sides between aristocrats and democrats. The simultaneous attachment of the American mind to these two conflicting
ideas promotes a fuller realization of the immensity of America's
continuing break with the past, precipitated by the Revolution and
kept fresh by the constant experimentation necessitated by the
task of building a new nation in a new physical and intellectual
environment. The duality of mind resulting from being caught half-
way between casting off an old ideological garment and donning
a new one can be glimpsed from the coincidence of events like the
following, which occurred at the very beginning of the nation.
Members of the Second Continental Congress hardly had time to
clear their heads of the echoes of one commitee report that announced that "all men are created equal" before turning to debate
the proposal of the Comte de Broglie that an elective monarchy
be set up. While the Order of the Cincinnati, founded in 1783 under
the patronage of Louis XVI, was preparing to build a perpetual
society of aristocratic Revolutionary heroes in which membership
should be transmitted through the eldest male posterity, the state
legislatures, following the early lead of Virginia, were preparing
to abolish the law of primogeniture. While the nation's press was
cheering to the echo of the fall of the Bastille (and, incidentally,
taking credit for it through American example), the First Congress
of the United States was debating "court etiquette," titles, and
whether President Washington should be provided with a throne.
From such beginnings the list could continue through the nineteenth century, as the few examples furnished under each half of
the paradox suggest.

In seeking an explanation for the stubborn persistence of this duality of mind, Dixon Wecter advanced the idea: "No one is more incurably romantic than a democrat, and we in America have fostered the legendary glamor of a Virginia peopled exclusively by Cavaliers fleeing the axe of Cromwell's headsman with their pockets stuffed with crested silver and a family portrait or two under their arm, a New York colonized by lordly patroons stepping off *The Little Sea-Mew* straight from Amsterdam with Indians genuflecting on the shore, and a Plymouth Rock on which was kindled the blaze of religious liberty to illuminate the world." As has been suggested, another explanation might be that the cutting of the knot that bound Americans mentally to the past was not as simple a task as that of severing the political tie. That the force of tradition took more than a century to lose its hold is not inconceivable, for old habits of mind do persist while new ones are being built, and their building is a slow process.

This explanation seems to be borne out by the campaign biographies. As was remarked, the one noticeable change in the pattern comes in the twentieth century. No longer do the biographers rail against the idea that one's ancestors are of any significance; they give them for what they are worth, with neither obvious relish nor apology. This change may be due in part, at least, to other reasons: the almost complete eclipse of aristocracy everywhere, especially after World War I; the repeated crippling blows that recent science has struck at the potency of heredity; and the fact that a combination of Hollywood competition and the income tax has dimmed the glitter of a well-ancestored Society and very nearly removed its members from the eyes of the admiring and inquisitive multitude. It may also indicate the arrival of a certain stage of national maturity. Traveler Mackay's keen observation of 1846, that Americans "as a nation feel themselves to be in the position of an individual whose permanent place in society has not yet been ascertained," has lost its validity. Perhaps by the twentieth century the American democratic tradition of individual worth has become a habit and a certainty in the American mind, and the American need no longer shout it and discourse on it as though he were striving to convince himself. Perhaps it is so taken for granted now, that the thought of being challenged as an aristocratic heretic because of a discussion of genealogy simply never occurs to anyone.

Regardless of its reasons for being, the ambivalence was recognized by the campaign biographers of the nineteenth century and was cleverly put to use. The candidate, like the voter, was said to disparage ancestral pride and hold that "a man's a man for a' that." Yet, as though he were a doting parent telling a sentimental, endearing incident from the childhood of a blushingly protesting adult daughter, the biographer adroitly imparts the information about the candidate's ancestors that he knows the voter will relish. For they are the sort of ancestors the voter either fancies he himself has or wishes he had: fugitives from tyranny, fighters for liberty, heroes from the Golden Age of the Republic. The biographer plays on the public-school memories of the voter, snatching from the pages of the textbooks the romantic patriotic impressions of Washington, Nathan Hale, Daniel Boone, and the Pilgrim Fathers and giving them the names of the candidate's ancestors.

Thus is begun the first step in the creation of a folk hero—sprung from worthy sires but scorning to trade upon them.

3

THE HAND THAT ROCKED THE CRADLE

The Parents of the Candidate

GENERAL LEW WALLACE, WRITING IN 1888, VOICED A CAU-
tion uncommon among campaign biographers. The American people, he observed, "know that good fathers have base children. . . .
In fact this is the American law of the case—well for the parent
if he have a worthy son, well for the son if he have had a worthy
parent." Much more prominent is the competing, and less generous,
bit of folk-wisdom contained in the proverb that formed a chapter
title for a campaign biography of William Howard Taft: "Like
Father—Like Son." Indeed, this biographer's explanation that "So
much attention has been given here to the characteristics and accomplishments of Alphonso Taft because this description of the
father is but a delineation, in part, of the son" might well serve
the majority of campaign biographers who present lengthy and
detailed treatments of the parents of the candidate. The dangers
latent in this idea have given trouble only once. Unable or unwill-
ing to paint Blaine's father in a very favorable light, his biographer
was obliged to insist that "Mr. Blaine's traits of character, which
have made him a statesman and a leader, are peculiar to himself,
and differ widely from those of his father. . . ." Otherwise, there
is a remarkably consistent stereotype of the candidate's father
present in almost all of the biographies. He is a respected member
of the community, generous if he is well-to-do (none are ever
wealthy), honest if he is poor, always hard-working whether affluent
or poor, always a model of civic virtue (yet seldom an important
officeholder), and well-beloved of his neighbors.

There is no ambivalence here, for the suspect word "heredity"
is not involved. This is a matter of the youthful candidate's early
association, the mental and moral climate in which he grew to

maturity. It is the function of the father to instill in the candidate, by precept and example, the heroic virtues of an ideal citizen of the Republic. The anonymous biographer of William Henry Harrison placed the matter squarely before his voter-reader: "Aware as every one must be, of the powerful influence of early education, it is worthy of remark, as well as gratifying to know, that a candidate for public office, in whom we feel an interest, passed all the early years of his life with the brightest examples always before him and under the parental tuition of one of those illustrious patriots, whose memory is revered by every true-hearted American. It is pleasing to know, that his first political sentiments were imbibed in a school of the purest republican principles. . . ."

Sons of heroes of the Revolution like Harrison and John Quincy Adams might be expected to have lisped "republican principles" from infancy. Indeed the biographer of the latter asked his reader, with almost indignant incredulity, "Could such a *father*, while he was hazarding fortune, fame, and life itself, in support of liberty and independence, instill into the mind of his son, principles adverse to the rights of man? Could *any youth*, brought up within the domestic circle of such men as *Samuel Adams, Josiah Quincy* and *John Hancock*, fail to imbibe a portion of that manly spirit of freedom which moved, animated, and prompted their every thought and action?"

But not every republican nursery need be equipped with a famous revolutionist in order to be productive of future statesmen. Indeed, they were the exception rather than the rule. Down the years and through the length and breadth of the land, it has been the nobly patriotic but relatively obscure fathers, the "embattled farmers," unsung individually, who have held the nation's destiny on their knee and have not failed it. From a father who was "a firm Whig in the Revolution," the youthful Van Buren heard "the maxims of piety, industry, economy, and patriotism" and learned democratic principles. An intrepid minuteman from the hills of New Hampshire taught his son Franklin Pierce "Patriotism, such as it had been in revolutionary days," and "no mode of education could be conceived, better adapted to imbue a youth with the principles and sentiments of democratic institutions. . . ." This instruction in civic virtue continues undiminished in the twentieth century. It has not been relegated to the public school system, but remains

27

the function of the father. Recreating the boyhood of Coolidge, his biographer wrote: "Remembering how to a son his father's pursuits are a constantly emphasized and meaningful actuality, and constantly provocative of imitation, here was a boy that was almost literally rocked in the cradle of political liberties. And this continuous experience was always being reinforced by the tradition from generation to generation of those who had not only carried on, within the family circle, the story of life-and-death devotion to their country in its infancy, but were continuously expressing a contemporary patriotic spirit."

The picture of the candidate's mother as evoked by the campaign biographer is just as consistent as that of the father. She is a model of Christian motherhood. In her, piety rather than the civic virtue of the father is the leading characteristic. Cheerful and devoted, she is primarily a homemaker. This classic picture is not Whistler's mother, but William McKinley's: "To see her," his biographer wrote, "you must imagine a bright-eyed, motherly old lady, dressed in soft black, with a white lace collar around the throat and a cap of snow-white on her head. She is straight, well formed, and of medium height, and her hair is the color of frosted silver and combed so that the white strands curl just over the ears before they are tucked into the snowy cap."

It is to the teaching of his mother that the candidate owes his strong moral sense, his unostentatious piety, and his purity of heart. Sometimes this was achieved by the patient industry of a Nancy Hanks teaching the young Abe to read the Bible; sometimes by example, like Blaine's mother who "unconsciously taught to all who knew of her Godly life that great truth, that real Christian life is in the heart and character. . . ." Such teachings leave an indelible mark on the candidate so that, like Jackson, he "never seems so cordially satisfied with an opinion, as when it happens to be after his mother's manner of thinking."

The candidate's mother really rises to heroic stature when she is widowed while he is still a child. Eliza Garfield, left a widow when James was still a baby, furnished his biographer with a superb opportunity for ladling up the syrupy mixture of pathos and romantic drama so dear to the late Victorian heart. "The influence of her chastening is upon her; it will be to her a softening thought and one to nerve her arm, for hers is a heroic soul—she comes from no common mould; she will come forth from the death-chamber well armed for the battle of life. In her veins runs the blood of the Puritans, and all the energy, intelligence and perseverance of that grand old race lies mingled in her frame. No danger it will fail her now; no danger but that such a woman will succeed; no danger but that such a mother is a fit woman to raise a President." Required to be both mother and father, the widow takes on the additional task of inculcating in the youthful statesman a sense of civic duty and an exalted patriotism. Thus Jackson's mother impressed upon her sons "as a first duty, to expend their lives, if it should become necessary, in defending and supporting the natural rights of man."

Despite the existence of a remarkably consistent stereotype of the character and function of the candidate's father and mother, there is a perceptible variation over the years in the biographers' treatment of the parents. In the early nineteenth century the tendency is to allot very little space to the candidate's parents—often a paragraph or two on each is deemed sufficient. By the 1850's the delineation of the parents is beginning to grow in detail. Since the Civil War the general trend has been toward an increasingly lengthy treatment.

The father has changed surprisingly little. As far as their character and function are concerned, the father of John Quincy Adams and the father of Calvin Coolidge are interchangeable. The one noticeable addition to the role of the father occurs in the twentieth century—he becomes the chum and companion of his son.

More pronounced are the changes that occur in the character and role of the mother. There is a slight but steady increase in the amount of attention given her since the Civil War. But more important are the amendments made in the stereotype of the mother. While remaining primarily a homemaker who keeps an attractive, happy, and morally upright household, she constantly gains in intellectual status and civic usefulness. Early biographers might remark on "her more than ordinary sagacity"; at mid-century one might be willing to concede that "she was distinguished for her masculine sense"; but not until the twentieth century do we find her, like Taft's mother, with "such an independence of character and thought as to make her an element to be reckoned with in any community where she might live." As the century wears on, the biographer comes to boast of mothers who have entered the learned professions. Huldah Hoover was a Quaker minister "by virtue of her spiritual insight, intellectual acumen and moral responsibility"; the mother of Wendell Willkie became the first woman to be admitted to the bar in Indiana.

The historian of the American family has noted the rather persistent observation of foreign travelers that there has been, at least since the Revolution, a singular absence of affection among the members of that institution. He somewhat reluctantly agrees that this observation is accurate, especially so in comparison to European families, and is inclined to agree with the foreign observers in laying the blame on the universal spirit of independence, the exhausting labors of frontier existence, and the great mobility that has been characteristic of American society. The campaign biographies attest to this lack of affection and looseness of family ties. Whether they dutifully acknowledge the parents in a paragraph or two like the early biographies or whether they run on for an entire chapter like the more recent ones, there is little by way of direct statement or oblique incident to indicate any lavish mutual outpouring of tenderness.

Instead, the emphasis in the biographies, from beginning to end, is upon the *duty* of parents to provide a moral and spiritual environment suitable for the nurture of a future statesman. If these campaign biographies enshrine the ideals of the American people, one obvious and persistent ideal of the American family emerges. The father provides amply for the physical comfort of the family by honest toil and, by precept and example, inculcates in his sons a love of country and a desire to render it service to the limit of their capacities. The mother devotes herself to making the home a cheerful, comfortable place in which to live and to making her children morally upright Christian men and women. Both perform their functions in a spirit of devoted self-sacrifice—the roles of patriarch and matriarch are not emphasized.

Compared to the amount of attention that historians have lavished on the church and the school in America, there is a relative poverty of historical knowledge concerning that most basic of our institutions—the family. The only scholarly attempt to chronicle the full sweep of its history is the pioneer effort of Arthur W. Calhoun, published forty years ago. This work concerns itself hardly at all with the ideal of family life, generally neglects the great emphasis on the duty of parents, and barely mentions the distinct and well-defined roles of each parent.

Yet the literature, fiction as well as nonfiction, of the nineteenth century teems with discussions of every aspect of these themes. An endless stream of books for the guidance of parents, bearing such titles as *The Parental Monitor; The Father's Book;* or *Suggestions for the Government and Instruction of Young Children on Principles Appropriate to a Christian Country;* and *Hints for the Training of Youth: A Scrap Book for Mothers,* poured from the nation's presses.

Contributors to the periodical press never wearied of emphasizing this separate responsibility of the parents. So seriously was it considered the duty of the father to attend to his sons' civic education that Dr. Benjamin Rush urged, as early as 1802, that women should be trained in order to instruct their sons "in the principles of liberty and government" since professional concerns often took men away from their families.[1] Indeed, this idea provided a good argument for the ladies' magazines that championed increased educational opportunities for women. "How extensive should be the education of females," *The Ladies Garland* stated editorially, "when they have such important office to fulfill—the office of forming for their country heroes to defend it, and politicians to guide and direct affairs of the nation." [2]

While the hortatory writers for American family magazines were willing to make this adjustment for the sake of father's business cares,[3] it was a reluctant concession. Mother, they believed, had her own peculiar sphere of operations, and they detailed her func-

---

[1] "Thoughts upon Female Education," *New England Quarterly Magazine,* I (April, May and June, 1802), 146.

[2] II (October 22, 1825), 147–48. See also "Thoughts on Domestic Education," *Ladies Magazine,* II (August, 1829), 385–89.

[3] Indeed few writers presumed to instruct the father in his duties. When they did venture a suggestion, it was usually in an article directed primarily to women and was often prefaced by a remark like, "Man's advocations in business, either in public or private life demand most of his time and attention; yet. . . ." *Lady's Monitor,* I (August, 1801), 19–20. See also *The Weekly Monitor,* I (September 6, 1817), 164; *Ladies Afternoon Visitor,* I (December 25, 1806), 13; "The Model Husband," *The Ladies Repository,* VIII (November, 1848), 334.

31

tions with monotonous regularity. How often women must have read articles that began "the formation of moral habits and principles, comes still more immediately under the mother's influence" [4] is reflected in one rather unique opening: "There are Mothers," the author ventured, "who will go with us through this short essay with no sneer upon their lips, though we say only what has been said over and over again." [5] Their duty was impressed upon them with morbid little "real life" accounts: "The solemn obligations that mothers are under to instill into the minds of their children the principles of purity and rectitude, and to discountenance and correct in the most prompt and unqualified manner, the slightest deviation therefrom . . . is illustrated by an account of a boy who was about to be executed after years of an 'infamous' life. He begged for his mother and when she came he bit off her ear, saying his career was her fault for her connivance at some trivial aberrations from truth and rectitude, during his childhood. . . ." [6]

Standing out in sharp contrast to threats of filial mayhem, another approach frequently employed was the apotheosis of motherhood. Women were flattered into the traces of duty by extravagant metaphors: "like a flower in some lone and unfrequented spot [which] sends forth a sweet odor to the chance passer-by, so does woman, from her obscure retreat by the fireside, send forth the sweet and holy fragrance of her influence upon man, and, calming his tempestuous passions, makes him a better and nobler being." [7]

Nineteenth-century "best sellers" provided an additional vehicle for these ideas. The perennially popular Mrs. Lydia H. Sigourney, in a nonfiction best seller of 1833, pounded her vast audience with the proposition that the mother should "render a noble service to

[4] John A. Bolles, "Influence of Woman on Society," *Ladies Magazine*, IV (May, 1831), 259. Their number is legion. Two gems are Caleb Atwater, "Female Education," *Ladies Repository*, I (January, 1841), 12–14, and Mrs. M. E. Doubleday, "The Necessity and Importance of a Well Directed Maternal Influence," *The Family Circle and Parlor Annual*, VII (January? 1849), 179–83.

[5] "The Young Mother," *The Ladies Companion and Literary Expositor*, XII (April, 1840), 253.

[6] J. S. Tomlinson, "On Female Influence," *Ladies Repository*, I (May, 1841), 135.

[7] "Female Influence," *Family Circle and Parlor Annual*, VIII (August, 1849), 401.

the government that protects her by sowing seeds of purity and peace in the hearts of those who shall hereafter claim its honor or control its destinies." [8] Even the saucy Fanny Fern, whose impudent essays furnished a genteel, "shocked" titillation for her wide audience in the 1850's, planted these ideas with due reverence among her *Fern Leaves*. She may have chided joyless piety and the stuffing of the young with dogma beyond their capacity to understand, but when it came to the stern responsibilities of a mother's role and the vital effect it has upon the formation of real Christian character, even Fanny played it straight.[9]

Best sellers in the field of nineteenth-century fiction furnish endless examples of mothers who could easily qualify to rock the cradle of a potential President. Not only do they match the characteristics of the mothers in the biographies but they are also conscious of their vital role and give lectures on it at every opportunity. For example, the heroine of *St. Elmo* (a novel which not only sold a million copies but gave its name to innumerable children, towns, streets, and hotels), "believing that the intelligent, refined, modest Christian women of the United States were the real custodians of national purity, and the sole agents who could successfully arrest the tide of demoralization breaking over the land, . . . addressed herself to the wives, mothers, and daughters of America; calling upon them to smite their false gods [woman suffrage], and purify the shrines at which they worshipped." [10]

To pursue the occurrence of these ideals concerning the proper functions of parents into all of the instruments of popular culture that have helped to shape the American mind would, of course, re-

[8] *Letters to Young Ladies*, 3d ed. (New York, 1837), 14. See also her *Letters to Mothers*, 2d ed. (New York, 1839).

[9] Fanny Fern [Mrs. Sara Payson Willis Parton], *Fern Leaves From Fanny's Portfolio, Second Series* (Auburn and Buffalo, 1854). See, for example, the essays entitled "Helen Haven's 'Happy New Year,'" 207–11, and "A Mother's Influence," 252–56.

[10] Augusta J. Evans Wilson, *St. Elmo* (New York, 1867), 404. See also Susan Warner, *The Wide, Wide World* (New York, 1851) and almost any of the several hundred such masterworks that issued from the hands of nineteenth-century lady novelists. Since a large percentage of heroines and heroes of nineteenth-century popular literature are orphaned in childhood, these responsibilities are assumed by their kind benefactors, all of whom admirably fill the mother's role. Note, for example, the character of Mrs. Linwood in Caroline Lee Hentz's *Ernest Linwood or, The Inner Life of the Author* (Philadelphia, 1856).

quire a separate volume. Schoolbooks, for example, throughout the nineteenth century, as a study of the famous McGuffey readers indicates, played no small part in instilling these ideals.

There is little doubt, then, that the ideal of family life in nineteenth-century America corresponded closely to the picture presented in the campaign biographies. There is, moreover, reason to believe that this ideal may have borne some relation to reality—at least prior to the Civil War. Testimony on this point has been given by numerous foreign observers.[11] But a basic change takes place in the realities of American family life after the Civil War.

It has become a commonplace among scholars who take notice of this phase of the history of the American family to record the decay of the traditional American family under the impact of the rapidly growing urban industrialism. The story of the breakup of the close-knit family group, with father leaving the home for work in the factory, mother emancipated and often also employed away from home, and the widening services of school and church in the training and care of children to fill the breach left by the absent parents, is a familiar one.

The campaign biographies do not reflect this trend. Indeed, they seem to indicate just the opposite in the growing amount of detailed attention given to both father and mother. In the biographies, both father and mother continue their historic roles in the rearing of the child.

The treatment of the parents of the candidate in the campaign biographies, then, presents a close reflection of the concept of the ideal parents in the society to which they were addressed. For the first half of the nineteenth century, they reflect both the ideal and what seems to have been the reality. In maintaining an almost constant stereotype of the father and an evolving stereotype of the mother, the biographies are again in close correspondence to their cultural context. For in our society, certainly the most striking advances in personal freedom and status have occurred through the evolution of the rights of women. Finally, the campaign biographies

[11] See Arthur W. Calhoun, *A Social History of the American Family from Colonial Times to the Present* (3 vols., Cleveland, 1918). This work, the only extended treatment of the history of the American family, places its major reliance on the accounts of foreign travelers.

and the realities of American society part company with the emergence of an urban-industrial America.

It would, perhaps, be a mistake to conclude from this that the biographers were simply out of step with American society, dealing in obsolete concepts, and unaware of the changes that had taken place. It might be much more likely that the sure political instinct which makes them such adroit propagandists has led them deliberately to ignore the real and to continue the old ideal. For there are many indications that America has done just this. Despite the seeming acceptance of the dictums of the new "sciences" of sociology and psychology on the theoretical level, and the growth of day nurseries, child-care clinics, liberal divorce laws, and the recent income tax exemptions for working parents on the practical level, these are still regarded as *remedies*, as second-best solutions to the problem of how to be a parent in an urban-industrial world. Whenever Americans discuss the ideal they hark back to the traditional American family. They have not been able to bring themselves to transmute their present practice into a new ideal of family life.

PART TWO: Youth

4

HOW DEAR TO MY HEART
Swimmin' Hole to Playing Field

THE CANDIDATE GREW TO MANHOOD JUST LIKE ANY ORDINARY boy. He was a model of propriety or a fun-loving young scamp, depending on the times; he was almost invariably bright, doing well in his studies but by no means a grind. Although his was a happy childhood, he trod no primrose path. For he was often poor, yet this was but a challenge which brought forth all his industriousness and ambition.

This attention to the childhood of the candidate has undergone a long evolution in the campaign biographies. Before the 1840's biographers devoted very little space to the events of the candidate's boyhood and youth. Most often the reader would be hurried from the birth of the hero to the outset of his adult career in an average of five pages. "Of the beginning stages of his life, we have no accounts, which particularize the character of his infancy," explained an anonymous biographer of Jackson. Only rarely would the reader be offered an apology for this indecent haste.

Gradually the emphasis on this portion of the candidate's life increased. By 1868 the space allotted to the youthful years of the candidate had grown to the point where it was felt an explanation was due the reader. One of Grant's biographers set the theme of this rationale: "As the child is father to the man," he wrote, "all the records of his early years concur in showing that he exhibited the same traits of character then as now."

In reconstructing the youth of the candidate, the biographers have become increasingly careful to show him as a lad who properly appreciated the necessity of mixing work and play. It would not do at all to have Jack wind up a dull boy. However, in order to prevent the cluster of images that go into making this highly nostalgic picture of boyhood from growing unduly complicated, it might be well to view the lighter and the more serious sides separately.

The lighter side of the early years of the hero provides an engaging succession of happy scenes that move from the simple delights of a barefoot childhood through the reputedly more sophisticated joys of giving one's all for dear old Siwash. Although this has long been the pattern, it was not always so. There is evident in the biographies a distinct evolution of play and a pronounced change in the ideal of boyhood.

Two ideals of boyhood emerge from the pages of the campaign lives. The two contrast sharply—presenting distinctly opposite ideals —and there is no discernible gradual shading from one to the other. From the 1840's to 1868 the ideal of boyhood is represented by a serious child of sterling deportment; after 1868 the closest approach to Tom Sawyer is the best boy. There are no "missing-link" boys in the biographies—no boy who tempers the model behavior of a little Lord Fauntleroy with mild prankishness.

The early ideal of boyhood would strike the present-day observer as not only a bit repulsive but also rather difficult to accept as operative on the level of practice. One can guess at the popularity of young Franklin Pierce, who was, said his biographer, "a beautiful boy, with blue eyes, light curling hair, and a sweet expression on his face. The traits presented indicate moral symmetry, kindliness, and a delicate texture of sentiment, rather than marked prominence of character. His instructors testify to his propriety of conduct, his fellow pupils to the sweetness of disposition and cordial sympathy." Yet Franklin might have been able to room successfully with James K. Polk, who "never missed a recitation, nor omitted the punctilious performance of any duty," or with Frémont, who "had not . . . the least appearance of any vice whatever," or even with Douglas, who "was universally beloved by all his companions . . . for his impulsive generosity . . . and the genial kindness of his disposition." The only future candidate who could have hurled epithets at this cherubic company was James Buchanan. He appeared as a mischievous youngster full of an "exuberant flow of animal spirits," thus breaking the completeness of the pre-Civil War pattern.

Only very rarely after 1868 does one encounter these paragons in campaign biographies. Then they are decidedly anachronistic and are due to the eccentricity of the biographer. The most superb specimen of the Lord Fauntleroy species, for example, was served up by that inveterate purveyor of platitudes, the Reverend Russell Conwell. Of young Hayes, he wrote: "During his attendance at the common school, he was always waiting at the steps of the old stone school-house when the door was opened in the morning, and never late in returning to his seat at recess. He did not splinter his desk with his penknife, nor throw paper balls or applecores at his neighbors. He never blew up the schoolhouse with powder, nor pinned streamers to the backs of his teachers. He engaged in no quarrel with his schoolmaster, and he strictly obeyed every direction and command of his instructors." Another biographer gives a very different account of Hayes's boyhood, emphasizing "his overflowing jollity and drollery more distinctly than his ardor in study."

The romping, prankish little barbarians that came to represent the ideal boy in the post-Civil War biographies might not have blown up the schoolhouse, but they did everything else. From the boy Grant romping with his horses, through Garfield tusseling on the deck of a canal barge, to the pranks of Cleveland, all that seemingly restrained total abandonment to mischief was the necessity for mixing their play with the hard work required to fend off poverty.

The twentieth-century biographers revel in their fun-loving subjects to an even greater extent. Taft's battles with boys' gangs demonstrated, his biographer felt, that "his beginning as a boy was healthy and normal." Coolidge took "the lead, in those mischievous pranks through which college boys cut the eye teeth of adventure." The fun-loving boy ideal reached its apogee in one campaign life of Hoover. For twenty-five pages Hoover chases rabbits, slides down snow-covered hills, plays Indian, fishes with a willow pole, and sports in the old swimming hole. By 1940 this trend had arrived at a point where the biographer of Willkie felt it necessary to protest that "chroniclers have been inclined to overdraw him . . . as a rebellious, hell-roaring . . . anti-everything young man."

From Tom Sawyer to Frank Merriwell is an easy transition and a matter of just a few years in the life of the candidate. This concern with the candidate as an athlete does not set in until the advent of Theodore Roosevelt, who although "nature gave him a puny body . . . by sheer will . . . made himself an athlete." Before 1860, biographers did not even mention the candidate's interest in exercise or sports of any sort. Beginning with Lincoln's wrestling match with Jack Armstrong, leader of the Clary's Grove Boys, until the opening of the twentieth century, the emphasis is on personal sports for exercise and amusement, rather than on team sports. Thus Hayes "allotted a due share of his time to hunting, as well as fishing"; Ben Harrison at college went in for "snow-balling, town-ball, bull-pen, shinney and baste"; and Cleveland's "principal exercise [was] driving." Far and away the most strenuous pastime was that of Horace Greeley, who "lifted weights at the Lifting Cure." "I have only lifted 265 pounds," his biographer quoted him as saying, "since I became sixty years old, February 3d last."

As noted, the real concern about the importance of the candidate's career in competitive sports appears in the biographies only in the twentieth century. Although he went to Yale, Taft did not follow in the footsteps of the great Frank Merriwell, much to the disappointment of his classmates, who had expected him to be "a tower of strength for the team." But he was a good swimmer and wrestler, and he accepted the creed of the believers in college sports: "He believed in athletics. He held it to be the duty of every young man to be a 'good animal' for this reason, if for no other, that it the better enabled him to do well in his work. The sound body was the foundation for sound work, and that was the main thing." Wilson "played a good game of baseball"; Hoover "made shortstop" on the Stanford freshman team; Franklin Roosevelt took an active part in football and rowing; Landon played end on the high school team; Dewey was a high school footballer; Eisenhower "was one of the best quarterbacks West Point ever had."

In the twentieth-century biographies the youthful athletic prowess of the candidates carries over into their adult life. They are said to maintain their interest as spectators in baseball and football and to continue to maintain "the sound mind in the sound body" theory by participation in less strenuous forms of sport. Golf is the usual activity, although occasionally there are deviations. Truman "enjoys a swim or a light workout in the White House gymnasium, followed by a shower and rubdown." Stevenson plays tennis and was previously so unplebeian as to play "squash a good deal at the old Harvard-Yale-Princeton Club." The exception to this great interest in athletics during the twentieth century is, as one might guess, Taft's 1908 opponent. Concerning William Jennings Bryan's views on sports, his campaign biographers wrote: "Exercise for its own sake is not included in the Bryan scheme of living." They add, unnecessarily, "To imagine Mr. Bryan playing tennis is preposterous."

No single picture of the lighter side of the ideal youth emerges from the campaign lives. Over the whole span of years from 1824 to 1960, the glimpses of the youth of the candidates provided by their biographers present a shifting pattern of ideas concerning behavior, play, and sport. Yet, this evolution has not been constant. Change has, rather, occurred in stages of varying duration. Thus the campaign lives reveal three distinct images of the ideal of happy youth. The ideal from 1844 to 1868 was a model child, interested neither in pranks nor in athletics. Between 1868 and 1900 it was a mischievous child, full of boyish deviltry, and fond of physical exercise and personal sports. Since 1900 it is the "barefoot boy with cheek of tan," a regular Tom Sawyer, addicted to organized sports and inordinately proud of his ability to "make the team." The relatively "youthless" candidates of the pre-1844 biographies indicate by their silence the existence of still another image—the ideal youth as one "seen and not heard." It is not inconceivable that this last might have been regarded as a *happy* youth by the adult population.

American society has long contemplated with awe and often with more than a little displeasure the evolution of childhood behavior. While it may undoubtedly be true that the first man to complain that "the younger generation is going to the dogs" was father Adam, no other society has had such legitimate grounds for complaint, for no other society experienced so rapid a transition from the belief that "children should be seen and not heard" to the "child-centered home."

From the early years of the Republic, foreign travelers marveled at the "indulgence shown by parents toward the excesses of children in earliest youth" and accounted it "one of the greatest evils of a Republican form of government." On April 16, 1827, the prospectus of the *Youth's Companion* heralded the beginning of its one hundred years of dedication to the instruction and entertainment of children with this statement: *"This is a day of peculiar care for Youth. . . .* Our children are born to higher destinies than their fathers; they will be actors in a far advanced period of the church and the world." The "new cult of childhood" was explored learnedly by an educational journal as early as 1833: "The attention now bestowed on children forms an interesting feature of the day. An interest seems to be rekindling, analogous to that which animated the ancient philosophers." And the cult's existence was attested to by numerous howls of protest and prophecies of disaster that issued from the periodical press. Historians have advanced the explanation that this early "emancipation of childhood" and development of a child-centered society was the natural product of life in a new country that looked to the future and labored for generations yet to come, and of a people who ardently believed in political democracy.

Yet if the precept that children should be seen and not heard met an early death on the level of practice, it nevertheless persisted as an ideal for a considerably longer period. No better index to the ideal of childhood can be found than the books that adults wrote for the edification and instruction of youth. Unfortunately, too few studies of this abundant literature have been undertaken. One of the best of these studies concludes that until the Revolution this literature reduced the child to oblivion, ceaselessly impressing him "with the fact that he 'was born not to live but to dy'" and that by 1835, although he had been acknowledged as a distinct personality and "humanely permitted a certain amount of legitimate pleasure en route to his heavenly home," he was still expected to be a model of deportment. The ubiquitous McGuffey readers, that for so long supplied the principal juvenile reading fare to so many, continued to press home their lessons of modesty, obedience, and disdain for mischief until the end of the nineteenth century.

Discussing the large share of attention given to boyhood in nineteenth-century American fiction, Henry Steele Commager concludes that "no other literature was so conscious of childhood or so indebted to it. . . . From Irving and Cooper to Howells and Crane, almost every major author wrote for children, and many of them mixed reminiscence with fiction to recreate, more authentically, the children's world." In this fiction for and about boys, one can follow the changes noted in the biographies from the model child to the mischievous, romping boy. There is as much difference between the youthful fictional audience in Hawthorne's *Tanglewood Tales* (1853) and Tom Sawyer and his companions (1876) as there is between the young Pierce and the boy Garfield of the biographies. On a considerably lower literary level, the same sort of comparison could be made between the heroes of Jacob Abbott's Rollo Series, the first of which appeared in 1834, and any of Edward Stratemeyer's syndicated juveniles—the Rover Boys Series, Motor Boy Series, and Tom Swift Series.

Periodical literature for children begins as early as 1802 and is very abundant for the entire nineteenth century. The evolution of the ideal of boyhood is particularly apparent in distinguished and long-lived juvenile magazines like the *Youth's Companion* (1827–1929) and *St. Nicholas* (1873–1940). The correlation between the heroes of this periodical fiction and the youthful subjects in contemporary campaign biographies is striking.

The campaign biographies thus follow the ideal of youth and to a certain extent reflect the real evolution of the status of youth. In this latter respect, the growing emphasis on the youth of the candidate in the biographies is the principal evidence. If it is true, as the testimony of foreign and domestic observers seems to indicate, that America was already moving toward the child-centered home in the first quarter of the nineteenth century, the biographies are out of step with reality. But by ignoring almost completely the youthful years of the candidate before the 1840's, the biographies seem to be nearly in line with the prevailing ideal that little boys should be seen and not heard, as expressed in numerous other vehicles of ideas from the school reader to the juvenile magazine. From the 1840's onward, however, the biographies keep pace both with the increasing attention paid to youth on the level of practice and with the changes that take place in the concept of the ideal boy.

The shading of boyhood into youth in the biographies is, realistically, a gradual one and, on the lighter side, is distinguished chiefly by a change in the nature of play. However, as the glories of the playing field come to eclipse the delights of the old swimming hole, they bring with them a set of values that leaves a permanent impression on the man. The athletic attributes of the ideal citizen of the Republic are perhaps of little significance when compared to the more profound qualities of mind and character with which he has been endowed. Yet because this attribute is but the concretization of the ideal of a strong body as essential to a strong mind and because this ideal has, in turn, had such a widespread influence upon twentieth-century America, it cannot be lightly dismissed. Moreover, few attributes of the ideal citizen have undergone such a complete evolution in the biographies and hence furnish such an opportunity to demonstrate their reflecting qualities as a mirror of social change.

As indicated, there is no mention of athletics or sports in the biographies prior to 1860. This is entirely consistent with the American attitude of the time.[1] Indeed, early in the century, according to one of the foremost historians of American sport, "It was generally believed that anyone who participated regularly in strenuous contests imperiled his health and courted serious injury." Summing up the interest in sports for the period 1830 to 1850, Carl Russell Fish writes: "American men were not devoid of the innate desire to develop and test their strength, but this was rather rural than fashionable and private rather than public. Abraham Lincoln became the chief wrestler of his community, but was not challenged by the champion of the adjoining district, and no one paid admission to see him." He adds that even "Shooting, trapping and fishing were, except in the Southeast, an occupation rather than a sport. . . . In fact, few American men had sufficient leisure for much participation in or attendance at games."

The transitional years, 1850–1900, witnessed an awakening of interest in exercise for its own sake and the beginnings of a passion for organized sport. Both of these aspects of athletic interest are largely urban in origin and are intimately connected with the rapid technological advances that came with the emergence of an industrial society. The sedentary nature of urban occupation, the nerve-racking noise and unlovely aspect of the mushrooming cities, and technological developments, especially in lighting and transportation, all combined to raise physical exercise, indoor and outdoor, to a new position of esteem. "All in all," concludes Allan Nevins, "the nation took a very different attitude toward sports after the war from that before. No longer could a man like Edward Everett deplore, as he did in 1856, the almost complete inattention to 'manly outdoor exer-

[1] Few topics furnish animus for acrimonious debate among both laymen and professional historians like the history of sport in America. Almost any generalization will summon a host of champions to enter the lists on behalf of a multitude of exceptions. The literature on the subject is abundant, contradictory, and wildly variant in quality. The generalizations offered here are, for the most part, from the only comprehensive attempt to record the social history of the United States, Arthur M. Schlesinger and Dixon Ryan Fox (eds.), *A History of American Life* (13 vols., New York, 1927–1946). For a discussion of the more specialized works on American sport consulted in this connection, see the bibliographical essay for this chapter.

cises, which strengthen the mind by strengthening the body.' " This is the aspect of athletics that is emphasized in the biographies from 1860 to 1900.

Although organized sport, team play, and the growth of spectator interest also had their origins in this period, the biographies do not begin to emphasize these aspects until they have become firmly entrenched at the outset of the twentieth century. As early as 1908 the pattern that persists to the present had been established in the biographies as it has become established in the national mind: give your all to make the team in high school and college; keep fit after college with tennis or, preferably, golf; and root for the home team and the alma mater as a spectator. The literature recording the rise of organized athletics and the growth of spectator sports is in solid agreement that it is only twentieth-century America that has become acutely sports conscious.

The candidate and his constituency have come a long way in a short time; beginning in opposition to athletics, they have come to number, among their most cherished ideas, an ardent belief in the value of sports.

5

MAKING HIS WAY
Life Is Real; Life Is Earnest

BEHIND THE CAREFREE DELIGHTS OF THE SWIMMING HOLE
and the glories of the playing field, there lurked some serious business to be attended to during the days of the candidate's youth. There was, for one thing, the very essential matter of getting an education.

Campaign lives that neglect the early education of the candidate are extremely rare. Except for those of Jackson and W. H. Harrison, even the biographers of the relatively "youthless" candidates of the period before 1844 paid some attention to their subjects' education. At least one biographer of John Q. Adams spoke of the boy's education as being interrupted by the war, adding somewhat too modestly for the erudite Adams that "although he was always of a studious turn, and addicted to books beyond the bounds of moderation, yet his acquirements in literature and science were all superficial, and he did not attain so profound a knowledge of things as he could have wished."

Candidates who received little in the way of formal schooling are spoken of as being "deprived" of an education, and their biographers feel it incumbent on them to explain why this tragedy befell them. Thus Van Buren left school at fourteen since that was the limit of his father's resources. Clay's widowed mother "did not possess the means to give her sons a classical education." Lincoln, Douglas, Greeley, Cleveland, and McKinley were all forced to forego the completion of a formal education. The biographers of these candidates not only elicit sympathy for this deprivation but take great pains to emphasize the manner in which their subjects made up for this loss by a heroic program of self-education. The reader is made to feel the deep pathos of the efforts of the underprivileged candidate to satisfy his thirst for knowledge as he plods "seven or eight miles" with Lincoln "to borrow a copy [of Kirkham's treatise on grammar]"[1] or drags himself with the young Greeley after a long day's work as an apprentice printer to the public library where "he spent nearly all his spare time."

There is, of course, a considerable amount of pride displayed by the biographers of these self-educated men, but it is pride in the ambition and capacity of the candidate to make up what seems to be conceded on all sides as a genuine deficiency. There is no insistence that self-education is the better way to learning, no attack on the regular processes of education, no sneer at the colleges or the college bred. Indeed, the trend is all the other way. There is a pronouncd adulation of formal education. Campaign biographers do not pass up a chance to emphasize the struggle of the parents of candidates to "get the boy an education." Like the father of Benjamin Harrison, they "sacrificed pride and personal comforts, everything, indeed, but honor, in the settled determination to see [their children] equipped for their several races." Especially was this true where the father "keenly felt the disadvantages arising from his own lack of education and determined in spite of difficulties almost inconceivable, to give his son better facilities for study than he had himself enjoyed."

The candidate, himself, of course, took the business of education seriously and very often worked his way through college. When Garfield learned that "a poor boy could get through . . . he then resolved to bend all of his energies to the one purpose of getting a college education. From this resolution he never swerved a hair's breadth. Until it was accomplished, it was the one overmastering idea of his life. The tenacity and single-heartedness with which he clung to it, and the sacrifices he made to realize it, unquestionably exerted a powerful influence in moulding and solidifying his character." Even the title page of one campaign life of Alton B. Parker promises "a full account of . . . his struggles with poverty and efforts to obtain an education."

As a student the candidate is always at least average. Quite often he is outstanding. No candidate ever fails. Interesting examples of

[1] Self-education reached a peak in the biographies of Lincoln. In his 1860 campaign life, William Dean Howells played it for all it was worth. In at least two of the 1864 biographies, it had already solidified into the form in which it has been handed down to generations of school children.

this are the elaborate efforts of Stevenson's biographers to explain why he dropped out of the Harvard Law School. One of them prefaced the explanation thus: "The story goes that he dropped out because of low grades. There is truth in this, but it is not the whole truth, and although correcting the story is rather painful to Stevenson for personal reasons, it ought to be done, since saying only that he flunked out of law school impugns his intelligence or diligence unfairly and calls into question his qualifications for public office, whereas the truth reflects neither credit nor discredit upon the man himself."

One of the most striking consistencies in the biographies is the great emphasis upon their subjects' popularity with their classmates. This urge to endow their subjects simultaneously with the democratic popularity of the average and with early manifestations of intellectual brilliance has resulted in the production of a formula that has been employed with great regularity. As early as 1844 an anonymous biographer of Polk recognized that "Habits of close application at college are apt to be despised by those who pride themselves on brilliancy of mind, as if they were incompatible." Thus the trick is to be an excellent student without being studious. One biographer of Coolidge even descended to the college vernacular: "Cal was no greasy grind." An exception, which incidentally emphasizes the alleged healthy normality of this formula, was Tilden, who "applied himself so closely to his books and gave himself such limited time for physical exercise that he broke down under the strain."

Although the candidates all turned in creditable records, the only subject that seemed to interest them was history. This special interest in history recurs in campaign biographies from Jackson to Eisenhower.

Except for history, it was the great teacher rather than the curriculum to which the candidates formed a lasting attachment. There is a pronounced trend in the biographies to single out a particular instructor for unstinted praise as the moulder of the candidate's youthful mind and character. During the Civil War, as Winfield Scott Hancock lay recuperating from his wound, he was visited by his old teacher, "Mr. E. Roberts." Weakened as he was, he struggled to his feet "to pay the respect due . . . to a good teacher." In the ensuing conversation, Hancock remarked: "I can never forget my school-teachers. I feel that my experience in life has proved this to be true: as is the teacher, so is the school-boy; as is the school-boy, so is the man." Sometimes it is the well-known teachers like Judge Story and Mark Hopkins who are the great influence, but more often it is the obscure ones like Coolidge's "Professor Garman," Hoover's professor of geology, John Branner, and Landon's "Uncle" Jimmy Green. When Hoover was Secretary of Commerce, he visited West Branch and gave his former grade school teacher a card inscribed: "To the real founder of character, Miss Mollie Brown, from Herbert Hoover, April 3, 1923."

To leave the impression that the campaign biographies glorify scholarship and cultivated learning would be, however, a serious mistake. True enough, they exhibit a solid esteem for formal education up through the college level. Indeed, they very often paint the candidate as a man possessed of a mighty intelligence. Thus we find that "Blaine was a real genius. He had exceptional mental capabilities"; Tilden's "intellectual resources are inexhaustible"; William Henry Harrison was "a great natural intellect." Through education the candidate, like Ben Harrison, "acquired the habits of study and mental discipline which have characterized him through life, enabling him to grapple with any subject on short notice, to concentrate his intellectual forces." This ability to concentrate his great mind upon a subject until he gains a thorough mastery of it is very pronounced; it springs from a passion for relevant information and a distrust of superficiality. Some even point with pride to the literary achievements of their heroes, their membership in literary and historical societies, and their honorary degrees. One 1952 life of Eisenhower tops them all with a listing of twenty-seven honorary degrees. Nearly all biographers insist on the ability of the candidate to express his ideas clearly and forcefully in a prose style of unusual purity. Thus Bryan's "style is as pure and captivating as that of Irving, or Addison, and not dissimilar to either." And "men most skilful in composition have utterly failed to imitate his [Grant's] style." A surprising number of biographers even admit that the candidate had a brief career as a schoolteacher. Pierce, Frémont, Blaine, Cleveland, McKinley, and Willkie "kept school." John Quincy Adams, Garfield, and Wilson were, of course, college professors.

There are, however, distinct limits. The candidate is a practical man. He has no use for "theoretical abstraction," no "propensity for metaphysical speculation," "no pride of intellect" to lead him to a "desire for display"; nor is he "deeply read in abstruse sciences." "Where others vaporize," wrote a biographer of Tilden, "he crystalizes. The realm of speculative philosophy has no attraction for him. . . . Facts are his friends and figures his delight." Some may have "thought him [Garfield] bookish and pedantic, until they found how solid and useful was his store of knowledge." Like Grant, "A President should not be a theorist or a book-worm. His lore should not be gulped down from musty books, where it was distilled full-flavored—and perhaps, poisoned in the flavoring—years, perhaps ages, before. It should be gathered, as the bee gathers its honey, in actual contact with men."

In short, it is not a little learning but too much that is a dangerous thing. The danger lies in the paralysis of action; like Hamlet he may be "sicklied o'er with the pale cast of thought," robbed of his common sense, and deprived of contact with reality. Few biographers have had to anticipate charges like this. One of the few admitted in his biography of Wilson that "A seductive solution of the problem to a man of scholarly tastes is to become a reticent, self-absorbed solitary." But, he hastened to add, "affability was hereditary with Wilson. . . . He was much too fond of social intercourse ever to become a scholastic recluse. . . ." The biographer of Wilson's 1912 opponent was "broadminded." Taft, he said, "believes in the 'scholar in politics' but not in the accepted 'scholar in politics' plan of activity. If the scholar can be persuaded to get down to rock bottom and meet the people of his district and associate with them in their political activities Taft believes that the result can only be beneficial to both sides."

The end of thought is action. The candidate has a tireless drive to acquire the facts, an immense capacity to assimilate the facts, an inspired ability to present the facts, and the good sense to act upon the facts. "Doers have ever been practical men," philosophized a biographer of James M. Cox. "But practicality need not, and does not, imply a lack of vision. There is such a thing as ideality in vision and a practical hand to make good the picture of the mind." "Parlor dialecticians," "so-called 'intellectuals,'" and "that glittering class known as Café Society," are the sworn enemies of the candidate (here, Willkie, Coolidge, and Dewey, respectively) because this "healthy respect for the facts" keeps him from being, like themselves, theorists or doctrinaires.

52

The process of acquiring an education is only part of the serious side of the youth of a presidential candidate. Mention has already been made of the hardships many encountered in securing an education, but the struggle to make one's way before reaching maturity goes much further and deeper than this. In and out of school the youthful candidates trod no primrose path. Their beginnings, at least most of them, were humble and their early life bears a marked resemblance to that of Horatio Alger's heroes. But there is no lamenting of these circumstances, no eliciting of pity. On the contrary, the biographers glory in the epic battle of the candidate against poverty and hold up his inevitable victory as an inspiration to youth and a vindication of the "American way of life." No one theme in the entire range of campaign biographies stands out more strongly and consistently than this "self-made man" ideal.

The opening of these epics of the cult of success is, appropriately enough, the birth of the candidate into a decent poverty. Cartoonists and professional humorists have amused the nation for some time with jokes about the importance of being born in a log cabin if one has presidential aspirations. Yet campaign biographers have far less to say about this than the popularity of the jokes might suggest. Indeed, there was no concern at all with the house in which the candidate was born until 1852.[2]

Only the biographers of Pierce, Buchanan, Lincoln, and Garfield could rejoice in the log-cabin birth of their subjects. But campaign biographers do not despair easily. Witness the case of the biographer of Hayes who, although forced to admit that his hero was born in a brick house, insisted, almost pathetically, that it had a log extension on it. If they settle for less, they insist upon the extreme modesty of the house. "The house is a mere shanty," wrote Oliver Optic, describing the birthplace of Grant, but "It was a good enough house for so great a man to be born in, and compares very favorably with that in which Lincoln, his co-laborer in the war, first drew the breath of life." Only rarely is the house described as anything but an "unpretending frame house" or an "humble cottage." While Franklin Roosevelt could not hope to rival his 1932 opponent, who first saw

[2] Despite the popularity of log cabins in the Whig campaign of 1840, it was not claimed that Harrison was *born* in a log cabin. He, allegedly, simply lived in one (with the latchstring out and a barrel of hard cider handy). As a matter of fact, none of the four campaign biographies of Harrison that have been used here even mentions log cabins.

the light in "a one-story cottage across an alley from Jesse Hoover's blacksmith shop," his biographer described FDR's birthplace as "the old family house on the ancestral farm."

Born in poverty or in very modest circumstances, the candidate embarked on a course which, although it lay inevitably upward, was a rocky one. Only his native ability, combined with his dauntless spirit and tireless industry, could overcome the numerous obstacles that littered the path to the summit. Ragged Dick and Tattered Tom meet their match in these "real life" stories. From 1824 to 1960 the readers of campaign biographies have waded through pages that would have been turgid with tears if they were not secure in the foreknowledge that grit and determination would triumph in the end. They embarked on life with Jackson, who "at the age of fifteen found himself alone in the world . . . divorced from every living being with whom he could sympathize as a kinsman . . ."; followed the fortunes of William Henry Harrison, whose father "left his children little other inheritance except his example"; and discovered the young lawyer Henry Clay "without patrons, without influential friends, and destitute of the means of paying his weekly board." Starting without money or influence, often alone and friendless, Lewis Cass, Frémont, Buchanan, Douglas, and of course, Lincoln made their way by their own talents and great quantities of hard work.

The post-Civil War period, generally thought of as the heyday of the self-made man, brings only an intensification of an idea long since firmly established. The scenes that depict the early hardships of the candidate become more melodramatic. The youthful Garfield "packed a few clothes in a bundle, and placing them on a stick across his shoulder . . . set out on foot for Cleveland. Amid prayers and forebodings, the poor mother had bidden him good-bye, and he carried with him her kiss and her blessing, as his only fortune." Grover Cleveland, as a three-dollar-a-week office boy, was obliged to walk two miles to work through the snow with broken shoes and no overcoat. "But he never intermitted a day." Bryan was pictured scrubbing the floor of Lyman Trumbull's law office. With the exception of Seymour and Hancock the list of post-Civil War performances of the Horatio Alger role is complete from Grant to McKinley.

The twentieth century has lost its taste for undiluted melodrama but not for the essential details of the early hard knocks of its self-

54

made men. Campaign biographers continue to delight in a Willkie who "drove a bakery wagon . . . was nine when he sold newspapers . . . sweated with threshing crews"; a Tom Dewey who sold magazines at the age of eleven; and an Eisenhower who peddled vegetables through the streets of Abilene.

Campaign biographers are never content merely to present these details of the success story; they insist upon driving home the moral. In these little philosophical essays that accompany the narrative of the early struggle of the candidate one may find a full development of all the component beliefs of the cult of success. The supremely confident individualism that lies at the core of the doctrine knows no period—it soared in Jackson, "an individual, [who] by the force of his own peculiar talents and energy, has raised himself from obscurity to the highest attainable summit of earthly distinction"; and it stays aloft in Eisenhower, who early came to know "that he was capable of continued growth as long as he applied himself to his work and heeded the dictates of his own conscience." A blessing rather than a disgrace, early poverty "was a challenge" to Eisenhower as it was to Grant, whose "misfortunes and his struggles against the cold current of poverty, were a necessary discipline and preparation for the man." The way to overcome poverty, the way to the top, is through "work—hard, persistent, undaunted"; it is, continued the biographer of Taft, "the only means man has of progressing beyond the dead level of mediocrity. It is the touchstone of genius, the key to all great success."

Hard work will yield these results because "of the marvelous opportunities of humble American citizenship," and Bryan's life, his biographer went on to say, "demonstrates once more, as in Abraham Lincoln's time, that to the man of conscience, brains, and courage, the highest walks of life are open; to which neither poverty nor obscurity is a bar." This, the reader learned from Garfield's biographer, "is the grandest principle of American life and American liberty," that the General, "beginning with no greater blessings than a sound constitution and a strong ambition . . . has risen to the top of the ladder, every round of which has been a merited elevation."

So seriously is this drama of the self-made man considered that the biographers of the few candidates born wealthy are considerably embarrassed and sometimes descend to ludicrous efforts to find some

55

evidence of hardship in the early lives of their subjects. Thus the biographer of Franklin Roosevelt described the privations of Franklin's life at Groton: "The Boys slept in dormitories. The alcoves were small and bare. There was one tiny window. There was a bed, a chair, a bureau. That was all. The walls were plain, naked. Few pictures were permitted. Simplicity was not new to Franklin; but this extreme was a little more than he had experienced. . . . he liked it."

Only one biographer has had the temerity to ridicule the application of this "grandest principle of American life" to presidential candidates. Noel Busch quoted Adlai Stevenson as saying: "My life has been hopelessly undramatic. I wasn't born in a log cabin. I didn't work my way through school nor did I rise from rags to riches, and there's no use trying to pretend I did. I'm not a Willkie and I don't claim to be a simple, barefoot La Salle Street lawyer."

It is not difficult to draw a composite picture of the serious side of ideal youth as it emerges from the campaign biographies. For there is a hard core of characteristics that persists from the beginning. Two ideas are central to this unchanging pattern: first, that the youthful candidate began life either in poverty or in very modest circumstances and rose to a highly successful adult career by dint of hard, unremitting toil, native ability, and a dauntless ambition; second, that in the course of this upward struggle one of his first concerns was to secure an education, for education was considered indispensable to future success, and no sacrifice to obtain it was too great.

When we turned with the biographers from this lighter side of boyhood and youth to face up to the grim reminder that "life is real, life is earnest," we found that the wisdom of the poet had not been wasted upon them. Here, in their sober approach to the business of getting an education and making one's own way in the world, the biographers stand deeply rooted in values that seem to have had an unshakable and unchanging hold upon American society from its beginnings until now.

Any attempt to relate the attitude toward education found in the campaign biographies to ideas contemporaneous with them in American society is almost a work of supererogation. It seems almost

56

axiomatic that American society placed a high value on education and made sacrifices to secure its blessings for themselves and their children. Tirelessly, we have been reminded that the education of the people is vital to the preservation of the Republic and the sainted names of Washington, Jefferson, Madison, John Adams, and a host of others in the hagiography of the Republic are invoked in support of this proposition. Along with the necessity for preparing future citizens for the responsibilities of self-government there has persisted the equally deep-rooted belief that, in the democratic climate of a land of boundless opportunity, education furnished, along with natural talent and character, about the only advantage anyone could command in promoting his economic and social advancement. Although these are the most weighty and the most consistently pleaded arguments, other reasons have been advanced in support of the high value Americans have placed on education. Over half a century ago William Graham Sumner, in *Folkways* (Boston, 1906), penned a cogent summary: "Popular education and certain faiths about popular education are in the mores of our time. We regard illiteracy as an abomination. We ascribe to elementary book learning power to form character, make good citizens, keep family mores pure, elevate morals, establish individual character, civilize barbarians, and cure social vice and disease. We apply schooling as a remedy for every social phenomenon which we do not like." In 1934 George S. Counts, surveying the social scene for the American Historical Association's Commission on the Social Studies, found this attitude unchanged: "Organized education," he observed, "has probably become one of the fetishes of the American people. It is now commonly regarded as a certain cure for practically every human ill, from marital troubles to international conflict."

The campaign lives reveal, however, another strain of belief about the value of learning that has an equally ancient pedigree. They set distinct limitations upon the *kind* of learning that should be regarded as valuable. They point to two pitfalls that beset the pursuit of knowledge: learning not only ceases to be valuable but actually becomes pernicious 1) if it is pursued for its own sake and 2) if it serves to alienate its possessor from the great mass of his fellow citizens. In the first instance the value of learning is restricted to the utilitarian variety; abstract and theoretical thought are proscribed. In the second the lurking danger of an antidemocratic élite is forestalled by the assurance that book learning is only one form of knowledge—and not necessarily a superior form.

Unhappily, the conclusion that these ideas concerning the limitations of learning are a form of anti-intellectualism is inescapable. Doubtless, anti-intellectualism and belief in the value of education were fellow passengers aboard the *Sarah Constant*. Already centuries old before the *Sarah* sailed, anti-intellectualism manifested itself in numerous guises throughout the subsequent history of the nation. It burst forth during the Great Awakening in the revolt against intellectualism in religion. It rode the circuit with evangelists who confirmed their flocks in their suspicion of the learned clergy. It poured forth in hundreds of frontier folk tales that drove home their moral of suspicion and distrust of specialized learning and the learned. And it took concrete form in the lax or, frequently, totally lacking licensing laws for physicians and lawyers, permitting nearly anyone to practice these professions.

Nor was anti-intellectualism by any means limited to the frontier. Business success, according to the formula given in hundreds of nineteenth-century success books, did not require formal education. Indeed, the success books regarded education beyond the elements of reading, writing, and ciphering as a positive hindrance in getting ahead in business.

Politicians of all parties exploited the prejudice of their constituents against learning and the learned. Denouncing one's opponent as an egg-head is not a recent phenomenon. Jefferson's Federalist opponents denounced him as an atheistic theorist. Jeffersonians in turn denounced the scholarly Adams as still another variety of egghead. Jacksonians denounced the intellectual pretensions of the Whigs. Of more recent memory is the torrent of abuse heaped upon the Brain Trust by anti-New Dealers of both parties.

Religious thought, frontier prejudice, business success formulae, and political invective are no more than a small sample of the areas of American life where anti-intellectualism has been evident. No historian has yet attempted to deal with American anti-intellectualism in all of its manifold guises. In 1954 Merle Curti outlined the monumentality of such a task in his presidential address before the American Historical Association. Although this was not the purpose of the address, it serves admirably for our purposes. With his customary

58

clarity and vast scholarship, Curti demonstrated how intricately anti-intellectualist patterns of thought have been woven into the fabric of our intellectual life from our earliest beginnings until now. Venture where he may, the historian of ideas in America will encounter them.

Once again the campaign biographies reveal an ambivalence endemic to American thought—a simultaneous attachment to an almost pathetic belief in education as a universal panacea and a deep distrust of thought and the thinker. For those who abhor paradox, a resolution has been frequently offered. There is no contradiction here, the argument runs; all that is necessary is to bear in mind what Americans ever since the days of John Witherspoon have believed to be *the aims* of education. And perhaps it was this common-sense philosopher who provided the earliest reconciliation between the high valuation of education and the undervaluation of abstract thought, emerging with a full-blown concept of utilitarian education.

For many this reconciliation, however enticing, leaves too much unexplained. Too frequently, in too great numbers throughout their history, Americans have given generously of their money and their time to the cause of learning in countless forms—from an endowment of a chair of philosophy to a subscription to a Chautauqua. The burden of proof is on them who would find lurking in all of this the blighting animus of utilitarianism.

Except for the years of the Great Depression, there seems to be no reason to question the universal acceptance by Americans of the other aspect of the serious side of youth found in the biographies: the ideal of the necessity of and the opportunity for making one's own way in the world.

That the saga of the self-made man is a persistent theme throughout the entire span of time covered by these campaign biographies should surprise no one. The opportunity to rise from rags to riches purely by dint of hard work, thrift, perseverance, and the cultivation of a strong and virtuous character [3] is at once the nation's heritage

[3] There are a large number of terms employed by intellectual historians to describe this idea: the cult of success, the self-made man ideal, the Gospel of Wealth, the capitalist spirit, middle-class ideology. While these terms are not interchangeable, having among them a wide range of inclusiveness, they all have this idea in common regardless of what additional meaning they embrace. In order to avoid the misapprehension that anything more than this simple idea is intended here, only the first two terms have been used.

from modern Europe, its persistent ideal, and, to a considerable extent, its actual experience.

The self-made man ideal came to America by way of inheritance from the Protestant Reformation. It was already deeply woven into the intellectual fiber of those middle-class Englishmen who were aboard the *Mayflower* as well as those who waved it farewell. It flourished in seventeenth-century America under the clerical aegis of such a worthy as Cotton Mather and found abundant fruition in the eighteenth century under the careful nurture of Poor Richard. It reached full flower in the nineteenth century, especially in the years between the end of the Civil War and the opening of the twentieth century. In these years the preachers of this gospel numbered among their ranks millionaire businessmen like Andrew Carnegie and John D. Rockefeller, eminent clergymen like Bishop William Lawrence and Henry Ward Beecher, popular publicists like P. T. Barnum and the lecturer Russell H. Conwell, journalists like Edward W. Bok, and popular writers like George Cary Eggleston, Elbert Hubbard, and Horatio Alger.

Every historian who has written about the ideal of the self-made man has also made it clear that it was no hypocrisy and that enough examples of dramatic climbs from rags to riches did occur in nineteenth-century America to make this ideal more than an idle dream. Had it been "nothing but hypocrisy," one concludes, "it could scarcely have outlasted the century. It was, in fact, not merely the philosophy of a few rich men but a faith which determined the thinking of millions of citizens engaged in small enterprises."

Nor was the cult of success a nineteenth-century phenomenon that went down under the impact of the growing social conscience of twentieth-century America or, at longest, persisted to that holocaust of dreams in October of 1929. It not only persisted into the twentieth century basically unchanged, but it has even survived the Great Depression to burgeon forth with new phrases—replacing "character" with "personality," "perseverance" with "will-power," and lightening the burden of "hard work" with "personal magnetism."

The campaign biographers, then, have struck a rich lode of precious belief here and, as has been indicated, they mined it for all it was worth. From 1824 to 1960 the biographers have told a story that has never for a moment of all those 136 years ceased to charm. When between 1868 and 1900 Americans seemed to relish the story with a heavy sauce of melodrama, it was served up to them in the pages of the biography. Present-day America, which still relishes the dish in chaster form, is no more sophisticated; it is merely calorie-conscious.

PART THREE: Soldier

6

AN INTERLUDE OF MARTIAL GLORY
The Candidate as Military Hero

AT LENGTH THE YOUTHFUL CANDIDATE SALLIES FORTH TO
face the cares and responsibilities of manhood. Yet almost before the
last echoes of the graduation orator's stirring clichés have died away,
it seems the Republic is beset by her foes and the young patriot must
hasten to her defense. His career, scarcely begun, is laid by as he
buckles on his sword. There follows a splendid little interlude of
martial glory.

From the beginning, campaign biographers have felt sure that
recalling the sound of the war trumpet from days gone by would
awaken a sympathetic response in the voter. The military careers of
the nineteenth-century candidates occupy far and away more space
in their campaign biographies than any other aspect of their lives.
This was as true for the citizen-soldier candidates as for the professional-soldier candidates. And it was true not only for the period of
the "bloody shirt" following the Civil War but also for the pre-war
period. It almost seems as though it were possible to fight through
the military history of the United States, battle by battle, skirmish
by skirmish, from the War of 1812 through the Spanish-American
War, within the covers of the campaign lives. There is not a single
sentence of pacifist sentiment in all these thousands of pages, not a
breath of indictment of war, hardly a criticism of specific wars.

The biographers of the citizen-soldier enjoy a unique advantage.
Basking in the self-sacrificing patriotism of their hero, called Cin-
cinnatus-like from the plow in the best American militia tradition,
they can revel in military glory to their heart's content. In all the
wars of the nineteenth century their heroes have harkened to the first
shrill note of the fife. Among the first to volunteer for the War of 1812
was young James Buchanan: "His country called for his services," ex-
ulted his campaign biographer, "and throwing his law books aside, the

stripling lawyer thus enrolled himself as a private soldier, willing to take any place if he could but defend the interests of his native land." When the Black Hawk War began, young Abe Lincoln "placed his name first on the rolls." Franklin Pierce, who had vowed "never again . . . to leave his family except at the call of his country, in time of war . . . was among the first to put down his name, as a private soldier" for the Mexican War. Refusing appointment to any civil office after Sumter, Rutherford B. Hayes "had made up his mind to fight. . . . With him war meant service in the field, danger, death, if need be: the same chances that the simple country lads, springing to arms all over the country by tens of thousands, accepted, invited, in a rapture of patriotism that now seems incredible." The roll of the drum had certainly not lost its appeal at the end of the century, for it summoned not only the Assistant Secretary of the Navy, Theodore Roosevelt, from "his young family, the infant with a mother yet ill at home" to "expose his life daily and hourly in the very forefront of battle," but also the candidate of the opposition— "one of the first who offered the President his service in the war for 'Cuba Libre' was William Jennings Bryan."

It occasionally happened that circumstances permitted even the biographers of candidates who were essentially professional military men to invoke this Cincinnatus image. Thus, since Grant was a civilian at the outbreak of the Civil War, his biographer could say with near accuracy that "he was called from his hides and 'findings' by the guns which battered down Sumter." This was in much the same spirit that an earlier voting public had been told that the War of 1812 had forced Jackson to abandon "the sweets of rural occupation" because he "was conscious of possessing great military talents and his patriotism would not suffer him to sit with folded hands." Even the lifelong professional soldier Winfield Scott, declared his biographer, originally joined the army in anger over European aggression and "thus he combined in his character the elements of a patriot soldier."

Having demonstrated his patriotism and devotion by springing to arms in defense of the Republic in its hour of need, the candidate goes on to deeds of valor that prove his personal courage and his native talent for leadership. Heroes were never out of fashion in the nineteenth-century campaign lives. The candidate always led his men into the thick of the fight, recklessly exposing his person amid

66

a hail of shot and shell. From the intrepid Cass, Democratic hopeful in 1848, who leaped from the boat to be "the first on Canadian soil" in the War of 1812, to "the Rough-Riders charge, with him [Roosevelt] at their head, through a rain of Spanish bullets, the men dropping by twos and threes as they ran," the stories of the candidates' personal bravery read like so many citations for the Distinguished Service Cross. William Dean Howells, Hayes's campaign biographer, described his hero's Civil War exploits with gusto: "He was everywhere, exposing himself recklessly, as usual. He was the first over the slough, he was in advance of the line half the time afterwards. Men were dropping all around him, but he rode through it all as if he had a charmed life." A playing-field-of-Eton spirit pervades these nineteenth-century accounts. One incident out of a hundred pages of the "intrepid bravery and exquisite coolness" of Garfield is typical of the whole. During a minor battle of the Civil War the hero found himself holding the balance; both sides were wavering; "he turns his eyes to the northward, his lips tighten, he pulls off his coat and throws it into the air and it lodges in a tree top out of reach, then he says to his men: 'Boys, *we* must go at them.' "

But for sheer melodrama the palm must go to one of the great masters of American letters. Perhaps the most unforgivable instance in the career of Hawthorne was this tale of the Mexican War which he incorporated into his campaign biography of Pierce in 1852. The setting is a battlefield meeting of Pierce and General Scott, the man who was to be his opponent in 1852. Pierce has just had a horse fall on him. (His Whig opponents maintained that Pierce fell off the horse, an accident which they variously ascribed to drunkenness or fainting at the sight of blood.) Badly hurt, he commanded his men to tie him to the saddle so that he might return to the fray: " 'You cannot touch your foot to the stirrup,' said Scott. 'One of them I can,' answered Pierce. The General looked again at Pierce's almost disabled figure, and seemed on the point of taking his irrevocable resolution. 'You are rash, General Pierce,' said he; 'we shall lose you, and we cannot spare you. It is my duty to order you back to St. Augustine.' 'For God's sake, General,' exclaimed Pierce, 'don't say that. This is the last great battle, and I must lead my brigade!' "

While on the whole the deeds of derring-do are choicest and more numerous in the biographies of the citizen-soldiers, the military careers of the professionals are by no means devoid of personal valor.

The voter was permitted to share the excitement of hand-to-hand combat with George B. McClellan, Lincoln's Democratic opponent in 1864; to thrill to the bravery of a beplumed Scott riding into the face of a murderous cannonade as calmly as he was to take his political defeat in 1852; and to marvel at the courageous devotion of the wounded Hancock, Democratic hopeful of 1880, who refused to be carried from the field.

But the quality of leadership of the ideal soldier is compounded of more than his heroism in battle. The worshipped leader, and this applies equally to the professional and the citizen-soldier, is good to his men and shares every hardship and rigor of the field with them. He is what today might be described as "the soldier's general," or the "friend of the G.I." This was true from the earliest period. During the campaigns in the Old Southwest, Jackson allegedly "treated and spoke to them [his men] as his children," "resigned his horse to assist in conveying the sick, and marched on foot in the ranks with his soldiers, partook with them their meager diet."

The biographies continue thus through all the wars of the nineteenth century, varying only in detail. "It was," wrote Lew Wallace, campaign biographer of his Civil War comrade-in-arms Benjamin Harrison, "a bitter cold night and Smock, a picket, challenged an approaching man. It was General Harrison. He had a large can filled with coffee, and when [the picket] asked him what he was doing, he said he was afraid that some of the pickets would freeze to death, and he knew some hot coffee would help the men to keep alive. . . . After leaving, the General (then Colonel) passed on to all the other pickets to cheer them with the beverage." It may be true, as Bryan's biographers claimed that the McKinley administration sabotaged his chances to be a military hero by keeping the regiment he had raised out of action, but this did not prevent him from filling the role of the soldier's friend. Languishing in a fever-ridden camp in Florida, "Colonel Bryan was at once 'guide, counselor, and friend' to his men, winning the almost idolatrous love of each and all of them. He gave lavishly of his meager funds to secure the comfort of the sick and maintain the health of the strong. His days and nights were devoted to the service of the regiment, and more than one poor boy, dying of fever far from the wind-swept Nebraska prairies, passed away holding his Colonel's hand and breathing into his

Colonel's ear the last faltering message of farewell to loved ones at home."

Needless to say, conduct like this on the part of their commander inspired such devotion and loyalty in the troops that they followed him cheerfully into the very jaws of hell, and many a tear coursed down manly cheeks at his leave-taking. At Teddy Roosevelt's farewell to his Rough Riders "the men who had not winced on San Juan Hill wept that day at Montauk." However, this is more than a matter of glory, sentiment, and inspiring leadership. The men these candidates led were, for the most part, militia. More than "thinking bayonets," as one biographer of Grant called them, they were also "voting bayonets." There is an acute consciousness of this fact in the biographies, and much care is taken to lavish praise on these patriots and on the glories of the militia system. Sometimes, especially in cases where militia are led by professionals and behave in a cantankerous fashion, it is difficult for the biographers to restrain their displeasure, but most of them do, with a sort of philosophical resignation. Thus, after belaboring the militia as devoid of the "slightest tincture of discipline . . . always more ready to give advice than to obey orders," one biographer of William Henry Harrison concluded that "freemen serving voluntarily out of a spirit of patriotism" should not be treated like "mercenary troops" for they "had talent, intelligence, and feelings of the most sensitive kind."

As has been indicated, in many aspects the treatment of the soldierly virtues of the candidates has been much the same whether they happened to be citizen-soldiers or professional military men. Yet even with this constant effusion of the martial spirit, the prestige of the professional soldier has seldom been high enough to trust to military renown alone to qualify him for the presidency. It was one thing to exult in the heroism of a Cass, a Pierce, or a Garfield spurred by patriotic devotion to leave his comfortable profession for a soldier's duty, for this was squarely in the militia tradition and evoked the image of the minutemen of '76. But it was quite another thing to fasten these ideals on men whose profession was war or whose major claim to fame had been of a military nature.

But the difference in the quality of the response to the call of country is a relatively minor disadvantage for the biographer of the professional soldier. He has a far greater one. Soldiering is but a glorious interlude in the life of the citizen-soldier. He goes on to complete the image, beating his sword into a plowshare, resuming the arts of peace. "War is not his profession," boasted a biographer of Pierce. "He becomes a soldier only when his country has battles to fight; and when these are over, he throws by his sword and mingles in the quiet duties of private life." Henceforth his only interest in things military is in securing legislation for veterans' benefits and perhaps urging preparedness.

Not only do the paths of peace lead where the professional soldier cannot follow but, presumably, because he cannot follow, his campaign biographer must face the supposed popular prejudice that is summed up in the withering phrase "great soldiers do not make great statesmen." Whatever degree of truth may attach to this prejudice and regardless of how widely it may have been held, the fact remains that the biographers of professional military men from Jackson to Eisenhower were enough convinced of its existence to expend a good deal of effort in an attempt to overcome it. There is, moreover, an interesting uniformity in their efforts to combat the prejudice. They do not dodge the issue. Meeting it squarely, they try to show that it arises out of an outmoded and misconceived idea of the nature of the function of a military commander. As early as Jackson's time, they were pointing out that *modern* warfare required that a general be more than a "mere military chieftain." Real executive ability, they contend, is called for in administering the affairs, both military and civil, of a theater of operation. They emphasize that the candidate has held vast powers which, during war, were almost without limitation and that never once did he abuse these powers or trample in arbitrary fashion upon the rights of either his men or the civilian population under his control. Finally, they drive a stake through the heart of the prejudice by pointing out that the immortal Washington was a military man.

Often, but not always, the defense of the soldier is in response to attacks by his opponents. The attacks, at least in the campaign biographies, profess love for and gratitude to the soldier for his heroic services *but*, as the earliest of them put it, "the hero in war, does not always prove to be the best leader in peace. The daring intrepidity which constitutes the brightest trait in the character of a soldier, might lead to ruinous consequences if displayed in the conduct of a statesman." Indeed, one of Clay's biographers adopted not only the reasoning but the words of Brutus: "It was," he said, referring to his opposition to Jackson, "not that he loved Caesar less, but that he loved his country more." Not only civilians, like J. Q. Adams and Clay, have played the role of Brutus. Garfield, who, like the noblest Roman, was himself a citizen-soldier, raised the prejudice against General Hancock, his professional-soldier opponent.

The defense begins with a flat denial that the soldier regards the presidency as a reward for his military services. Rather than presenting his bill for gratitude, the professional is offering his gift of ability. His preparation for the office has been of the finest. It begins at West Point, where, the biographer of Grant assured the voter, "it is an error to suppose that our future officers are instructed only in what pertains to war as a theory and an art— their preparation for civil affairs is as thorough and complete as that of the student in our colleges, or the lawyer in our towns." His subsequent career builds upon this solid foundation, promoting as it did for Scott,[1] "two qualities, which belong only to minds of the highest executive order . . . the *sagacity* to foresee what means and instruments are required to fulfill the end and the *judgement* to select the *proper men* to use those means and instruments." A tour of duty as a quartermaster is "his commercial college, where he acquired," as Grant did, "business habits and training." It seemed perfectly obvious to Hancock's biographer that "the rigid economy, and the severe methods of administration, and the exact system incident to the profession of arms, render it an admirable training-school for the executive head of the civil department of the government."

But the defenders of the professional were not content to rest their case upon the presentation of the fitness of their candidate for the highest civil office. They were aware, as the biographer of Scott put it, that "In Republican governments, the people are naturally jealous of military power." The vision of things to come conjured up by Jackson's opponents in 1824 may well have served to reinforce an already deeply rooted fear. Hardly a better picture

[1] Scott was not himself a West Pointer, but for all of his long career he was an ardent champion of the Academy and especially of the kind of training that the biographers claim it imparts.

of that vision can be found in the speeches of his opponents than the one that his own 1832 biographer penned in a mood of exultant vindication: "He has now administered the government for nearly three years, and has shown nothing of the disposition to act the military chieftain. No gens d'arms guard his door, no halberdiers his person. He has never yet amused the good citizens of Washington with a military execution, himself preceded by laurelled lictors with their faces [*sic*] and axes, and with the *master* of the *horse* at his heels. If the apprehension of those who foretold such things were honest, they are happily disappointed."

As a consequence of their awareness of this suspicion of the military, biographers of professional soldiers repeatedly reassured the voter. William Henry Harrison, it was solemnly affirmed, although he enjoyed vast powers, "the most extensive since the Revolution," never once "transcended the respect he owed the laws, or abused in any way the high trust thus confided to him." Scott "was the servant of the laws, the faithful citizen, and the pacificator of troubled communities." With Grant there could not "be any reasonable apprehension, that, as a civil ruler he will transcend any constitutional limitations, when, with no restraint upon his authority but his own will, and wielding in full plenitude absolute dominion, he has uniformly governed public enemies with moderation and forbearance."

If after all these assurances there remains any lingering doubt, it is allayed, as has been indicated, by reminding the voter that the noble Washington was a military man. This invocation of the name of Washington in this connection requires little elaboration; it is patently too good a clincher for the biographers to miss. One of them insisted that "Washington himself was a *professional* soldier." Another even dragged him down from Olympus to make his point, claiming that the great Washington was guilty of trespassing on civil liberties but was cheerfully forgiven since his actions, like Jackson's, were necessary.

When Theodore Roosevelt went off to hunt lions in Africa, the curtain fell on the long first act of the saga of the candidate as military hero. It was not to rise again until 1952. The guns of Château-Thierry and Belleau Wood do not echo through the pages of post-World War I campaign lives as did those of Buena Vista and Gettysburg. This is not because the candidates saw no military service. Alf Landon served in World War I as a first lieutenant in the chemical warfare service. "On the day the United States entered the World War Wendell Willkie enlisted. . . ." Harry Truman was a captain of artillery in France during World War I. But that is all. There is hardly more than a sentence beyond these mere mentions.[2]

When in 1952 the professional soldier again entered the political arena, much that is reminiscent of the nineteenth-century biographies returned. There was the same grappling with the supposed prejudice against the military man, leading to the same insistence on his civilian-mindedness and the same denial that he was a mere military chieftain, the same attempt to show the pertinence of his prepara- tion, and even the same final appeal to the example of Washington. But the blood and the glory had gone. Instead came a new note: "There is no glory in battle worth the blood it costs." The candidate is said to "talk about the 'crime' and 'waste' of war and its 'beast- liness.' "

From the beginning there have been, of course, candidates who had not been soldiers. The apologetic manner in which campaign biographers have treated their failure to serve reinforces the con- clusion that military service is a valuable asset to the candidate. "Largely, it seems," explained the biographer of James M. Cox, Democratic candidate in 1920, "because no war came along when he was free of family responsibilities, Governor Cox has no martial record. He might have been a soldier of the Roosevelt type had he lived in other circumstances." Sometimes Congressional or state services on behalf of the war effort are praised as the neces- sary counterpart to the efforts of the men in the field. Dewey's labor as the first chairman of the USO drive has an element of the heroic about it, including as it did standing in chow lines, sleeping in tents, and taking open-air showers with the troops. Sometimes, like Franklin Roosevelt, they were confined to their desks much against their will. During World War I the young Assistant Secretary of the Navy "longed to ship to sea and active service. As an ordinary seaman! Persistent rumors that he had actually resigned to enlist in the Navy echoed and re-echoed in the capital." But perhaps the

---

[2] At least one biography of Truman provides an exception to this generaliza- tion. However, while it runs on at considerable length about Truman's military service, it is decidedly different in tone from the nineteenth-century biographies.

supreme example of the creation of virtue out of necessity occurred in one biographer's handling of Cleveland's patriotic response to the call of fife and drum. When the draft summons came, he wrote, "There was no question at all of what his duty was; he promptly supplied a substitute."

In the over-all view, the conclusion is inescapable that nineteenth-century campaign biographies were suffused with the martial spirit. But this quality is entirely distinct from militarism. These biographies teem with detailed descriptions of battles and they glorify the soldier. But the image of the ideal soldier that emerges from these gory pages is a citizen-soldier, summoned from his peaceful pursuits to save the Republic in her hour of need. Responding to the call with patriotic fervor, he performs valiant and heroic service, mindful always that he leads no band of mercenaries but citizens like himself; and when the enemies of the Republic have been scattered by the last glorious charge, he dutifully gives thanks to a just Providence and beats his sword into a plowshare. Any other sort of soldier will not do. Biographers of the professional-soldier candidate must somehow contrive to fit their candidate into this mold. Defensively, they must show that beneath that glittering uniform there beats a pure civilian heart, that the hand that held the sword can also wield the pen, and that the great principle of the Republic that subordinates the military to the civil authority finds no stouter champion.

By 1908 the martial spirit has departed the pages of the campaign lives and it has not yet returned. The biographers of Eisenhower were haunted by the ancient ghost of the supposed prejudice against military men and they broke the same old lances jousting with it, but there the similarity to nineteenth-century biographers ends.

This recurrent appeal to the image of the citizen-soldier as a cultural ideal and the development of a stereotyped defense of the professional are somewhat remarkable phenomena to encounter in the history of a professedly peace-loving people. And when it is recalled that nine of the major party candidates for its highest office have been professional soldiers, thirteen have been citizen-soldiers proud of their feats of arms, and most of the remaining twenty-two candidates have apologized for having missed an opportunity to display their valor, it could provoke the lifting of a cynical eyebrow at American protestations of their peace-loving nature. But if untempered, this would be too harsh a judgment. For nothing flows more purely from these fountains of political folklore than the conviction of these campaign biographers that they were appealing to a people who, although hardly deficient in martial spirit, abhorred militarism. The image of the ideal soldier shaped by the nineteenth-century campaign biographers is a product of one of the most persistent of American ideas—the distrust of standing armies. The recognition of the existence of this prejudice is essential to an understanding of the conscious inferiority of the professional soldier and the prideful assurance of the citizen-soldier. It provides the key to an understanding of this aspect of a people who at one and the same time abhor militarism and preserve the martial spirit.

The traditional distrust of standing armies has its roots in the seventeenth-century struggle between Parliament and the Stuart kings. Indeed, control of the sword to prevent its use as an instrument of executive despotism was as essential in British constitutional development as the closely related struggle for control of the purse.

Their colonial experience tended to fortify the transplanted Englishmen in their prejudice. This colonial aversion to the military came to a head in 1765 when bodies of Redcoats were quartered in American cities and provided the New England patriots with a splendid opportunity to exploit the propaganda value of this "vivid example of tyranny."

Even before the emergence of the nation, this fear of standing armies had found expression in the clear enunciation of the principle of civil control of the military. The First Continental Congress declared on October 14, 1774, that a standing army "in times of peace without the consent of that colony in which such an army is kept, is against the law." And two of the counts in the indictment of George III contained in the Declaration of Independence charge that: "He has kept among us in times of peace, Standing Armies, without the consent of our legislatures," and "He has affected to render the military independent of and superior to the civil power." The Virginia Bill of Rights in the same year provided the classic statement: "Standing armies in times of peace should be avoided as dangerous to liberty, and . . . in all cases the military should be under strict subordination to, and governed by, the civil power."

After the Revolution the Continental Congress legislated away the army that had won the nation's independence, prefacing the act with the well-established reasoning that "standing armies in times of peace are inconsistent with the principles of republican governments, dangerous to the liberties of a free people, and generally converted into destructive engines for establishing despotism."

The Constitutional Convention, locked in a vigorous debate over the powers of Congress to raise and support armies, listened to the same arguments. "The people," warned Elbridge Gerry, delegate from Massachusetts, "were jealous on this head" and, he continued, he himself believed "a standing army . . . dangerous to liberty, [and] unnecessary even for so great an extent of country as this." While the need for a standing army won recognition in the completed Constitution, it was not an unqualified victory. The old fear is reflected in the proviso that "no appropriation of money to that use shall be for a longer period than two years." The records of the debates in the state conventions called to ratify the Constitution are indicative of the hostility with which even this tempered provision was received.

From the debates in the Constitutional Convention and in the state ratifying conventions, one idea stands forth that is of prime importance to this discussion of the American attitude toward the military. Hostility to the maintenance of standing armies in time of peace does not stem from pacifistic sentiment. The foes of the standing army did not propose to leave the infant United States defenseless. They simply believed that the militia was both adequate for the task and above suspicion as a threat to liberty. Representing this belief was James Madison's argument in the federal convention that "the greatest danger to liberty is from large standing armies, it is best to prevent them by an effectual provision for a good militia." This faith in the citizen-soldier was eventually embodied in the same article of the completed Constitution that provides for a standing army.

Providing variations on this theme, delegate after delegate in the ratifying conventions of the various states testified to the belief in the adequacy of the militia. "We fear no foe," a typical advocate proclaimed. "If one should come upon us, we have a militia, which is our bulwark. Let Lexington witness that we have the means of defense among ourselves." Illustrating his point that the militia "will be such a bulwark of internal strength, as to prevent the attacks of foreign enemies," another delegate declared: "I have been told, that about the year 1744, an attack was intended by France upon Massachusetts Bay, but was given up on reading the militia law of the province." It need only be pointed out as an indication of the response to the temper of these ratifying conventions that the Bill of Rights provides, in Amendment II, that "A well regulated militia, being necessary to the security of a free state, the right of the people to keep and bear arms shall not be infringed."

Thus, from the earliest times the American attitude has been to distrust the military, to fear standing armies as a threat to liberty, and to believe that the maintenance of this attitude would not leave them defenseless because there stood, ready to spring to arms, countless thousands of citizen-soldiers who comprised the militia of the several states.

The use of the term "adequate" should not lead to the assumption that this reliance on militia has been regarded as a militarily inferior substitute made necessary by the attitude toward the professional military. Quite the contrary is true. The birth of this belief in the *superiority* of the citizen-soldier occurred on one June afternoon in 1775 when a rag-tag, bobtail bunch of citizens engaged British regulars on Bunker Hill and won a bloody moral victory. Here was the proof—battle tested. Bunker Hill made an ineradicable impression upon the thinking of Americans and laid the cornerstone for an American philosophy of defense that has lasted into the present. And if the philosophy needed reinforcing, it received it in that most inglorious of American wars, the War of 1812. The bloody slaughter at New Orleans of England's finest, Wellington's Peninsula veterans, by a motley group of militia and hastily armed citizens is certainly one of the cornerstones in the building of the legend of the citizen-soldier's invincibility.

A tradition so auspiciously begun has not been allowed to languish. In vain might professional soldiers point to its dangers. In vain might military historians seeking to attack the tradition at its roots point to the deflating facts that the entrenchments so vital to the successes at Breed's Hill (not really Bunker Hill at all) and

New Orleans were built under the direction of professional army engineers. The danger and the unreality are alike ignored. The schoolbooks and the popular accounts continually indoctrinate each succeeding generation in this peculiarly American brand of the martial spirit. Even after what should have been the sobering experience of World War I, an influential magazine applauded as "true statesmanship" a statement by an undersecretary of state that "Every nation needs an army for internal police purposes but beyond this every soldier is a potential offensive force."

Scorning the prophets of disaster, the nation once more pressed to its bosom the old tradition the undersecretary had dusted off and clung to it passionately in the period between the two world wars. And just a few years ago, Henry Steele Commager, attempting to explain Americans to themselves in an excellent volume entitled *Living Ideas in America,* dwelt lovingly on this "amateur spirit" and offered as a consoling thought to those who worry about the future that, after all, we have always won.

Against this background of the American martial spirit, it is not surprising to find that political opinion-makers have created their military heroes in the image of the citizen-soldier. Perhaps the valiant deeds of presidential aspirants will never be sung again as they were by the nineteenth-century bards, for this seems to be the only real change that time has wrought. The bitter disillusionment over the outcome of "the war to end all wars" may continue to be poisonous to the most gallant heroism within the power of any campaign biographer to chronicle. But essentially the image remains intact. Writing on the problems faced by a democracy standing under arms on the eve of Pearl Harbor, Pendleton Herring, an astute observer of the American scene, presented an admirable picture of the American military hero that could stand today with the addition of only one more name.

> In this country a persistent suspicion of militarism, joined with the feeling of security from threat of foreign attack, has served to reduce the influence of military men. We have been ready to honor military heroes but unwilling to extend admiration to the professional soldier. Our ideal is still the citizen who springs to arms in order to defend his country but who returns to his plow, his machine, or his desk as soon as the danger has past. Washington is revered not so much for his victories as for his great

renunciation of power and office. He stands as the Cincinnatus of our republic. Jackson was acclaimed not as a professional soldier but as a general who never lost the common touch. He was the common man in uniform. General Harrison, who commanded in the Battle of Tippecanoe, was presented as a hero content to sit before his cabin door and armed only with a jug of hard cider. Grant was the bluff, untidy figure who emerged from obscurity and made good where professional soldiers of established reputation had failed. Our military heroes have served to foster the faith that the civilian can become a soldier by reaching for his rifle. Theodore Roosevelt fondly believed that his experience with his Rough Riders qualified him for leading a division in the World War. His pretensions were not laughed away, for too many citizens could appreciate his attitude of mind. Teddy dramatized an approach to military problems which was widely shared.

PART FOUR: Apprenticeship for Statecraft

7

BENEATH HIS FIG AND VINE

The Candidate as Farmer

HIS BRIEF BUT SPLENDID HOUR OF MARTIAL GLORY ENDED, the candidate resumes the career he had abandoned in patriotic haste. At this point it would be logical to expect the campaign biographies to exhibit a considerable amount of diversity. In the private pursuits of their adult careers presidential candidates have followed the law, the academic profession, journalism, and a variety of business enterprises. It is therefore all the more striking to discover in the handling of this phase of their lives a considerable amount of uniformity.

The major unifying theme that is all-pervasive, regardless of the specific profession under discussion, is that the career of the candidate in private life has been a marvelous apprenticeship for statecraft. The skills he has learned, the knowledge he has gained, the habits he has acquired, in brief, the way of life he has followed in the practice of his private calling has provided him, almost providentially, with the very sort of equipment necessary to conduct the high office to which he has been summoned.

As the tableau of the apprenticeship for statecraft unfolds, two dominant roles emerge. One is a traditional part bathed in the mellow glow of a worshipped past, the other belongs to an unchanging present. In the first, a bucolic idyl of republican virtue, the candidate appears in the guise of the sturdy yeoman; in the second, a real-life drama of the world of affairs, he plays the role of the persistent American folk hero—the successful businessman.

The frequent use that has been made of the Cincinnatus image in discussing the candidate as a military hero is a purposeful one arising out of the materials of this study. No other historical comparison has seemed so eminently fitting to the campaign biographer, and his use of it, both explicitly and by inference, has been extensive. Yet the appeal of the ancient Roman lies not in his military skill (indeed, the crisis in which his modern counterpart is summoned is often not a military one) but in the fact that he was called from the *plow*.

From the time of Jackson to the present, the voter has been assured that almost every major party candidate was a son of the soil. To dismiss this fact as merely an appeal to the farm vote would be a decided oversimplification. The evokers of the Cincinnatus image are aware that their appeal is far wider than a simple identification with a portion, however large it was and still is, of the voting public. The biographers are convinced and it is generally believed, with good reason, that the appeal of the sturdy yeoman, the simple republican farmer, as a symbol of honesty, integrity, instinctive democracy, and almost mystical capacity for statesmanship is deeply rooted in the fiber of the American mind and constitutes therefore a continuing political asset.

Although the biographers unquestionably accept this ancient belief that the noble occupation of farming affords a splendid, even an idyllic, apprenticeship for statecraft, they have sometimes been hard put to establish their heroes' connection with the soil. For, despite the fact that the nation was predominantly rural through the nineteenth and into the twentieth century, few candidates could really be considered primarily farmers in private life. Yet it is equally true that very few of them did not engage in some agricultural work at one time in their careers.

Indeed, prior to the Civil War campaign biographers took it for granted that their hero had spent some years in rural occupation. Only rarely does one come across even brief mentions of these candidates' early agrarian pursuits. When they do occur, they are simple, straightforward statements like "Zachary Taylor was reared by his father to his own profession—that of a farmer; and until his majority, was practically engaged in it. . . ." Howells, campaign biographer of Lincoln in 1860, was not only similarly laconic but downright heretical in the handling of young Abe's farm life. "The work done," he wrote, "was in the course of farm labor, and went to the development of Mr. Lincoln's muscle. Otherwise it is difficult to perceive how it affected his career."

But after the Civil War the treatment of the candidate's roots in the soil becomes increasingly lengthy and increasingly less casual. Grant's biographers treat not only his youth on the farm but also his brief return to farming after his resignation from the army in 1854. "He built a house of hewn logs, working on the structure with his own hands," writes one of them, "thus drawing upon the experience he had acquired in his youth. . . . He was not above his business, nor in any sense one of those dandy agriculturists called 'gentlemen farmers'. . . ." This dig at "gentlemen farmers" was directed at his Democratic opponent, Horatio Seymour, who ran a large experimental farm and who was being advertised by his partisans as the "proudest specimen of American yeomanry."

Certainly by 1876 there is a clearly discernible sensitivity to the necessity of watering these roots in the soil. Irked by the manner in which his "candidate has been painfully contrasted with the agricultural simplicity of Mr. Tilden," the biographer of Hayes felt constrained to relate a rather pathetic little tale of how young Rutherford's mother felt impelled to keep him from going to Yale because the rusticity of his dress and manner might cause him embarrassment.

One could follow Garfield, Ben Harrison, and Bryan through their round of youthful chores on the farm, but it would accomplish little to pile up the evidence given by their biographers to establish them as genuine "country boys." Most of it is not strained; their farm origins were genuine enough. From the 1920's to the present, however, the treatment of the candidates' early lives on the farm becomes very nostalgic—the scenes of plowing, planting, and chores come to read like second-rate pastoral verse—and invites the suspicion that more and more is being written about less and less. The scenes of Hoover's days on an Iowa farm are so replete with the stock phrases for conjuring up bucolic idyls that one can almost smell "the meadow sweet with hay." (He was, after all, running against the first indisputable "city slicker.") But Republicans are no better at this conjuring than Democrats. In 1948 the voter was permitted "to ride along on the Emerson gang plow [with Truman], holding the levers with his hardened hands, while the earth curled in a black, sweetly fresh ribbon at the side of the shining steel moldboard."

One can almost sense a conscious grasping at straws, and this strain sometimes leads to slightly ludicrous attempts to give a ring of authenticity by supplying detail. Thus the voter was assured that Coolidge "could get an exceptional amount of sap out of a maple tree." And Truman, his biographers proudly record, was "an expert in the surgical art of castrating pigs." But doubtless the voter's credulity was most severely wrenched by protestations like this one: Franklin Roosevelt was being interviewed, reported his biographer, and was asked about his estate. " 'It's not an estate,' replied F.D. with an expression of annoyance. 'It is a farm. . . . Must our farm be called an estate merely because I'm governor, or because it's been in the family a long time, or because there are flower gardens there? . . . Call it by its right name—a farm. I don't like estates and I *do* like farms. . . .' A farm where thousands of trees grew. A place of corn fields. A place of rye fields and of chickens and cows. Potato patches, barnyards. . . . A place where F.D. himself, in years before the infantile paralysis, had gone to the fields and kept close to the realities of the soil and the life it nurtured." In 1908 even the biographers of Bryan had had to be careful with this distinction between a farm and an estate.

On the other hand, the small size of the "farm" has sometimes proved a source of embarrassment in establishing the candidate's early roots in the soil. John W. Davis' folks lived in town but the voter was assured that he still had to do the chores. "The cows had to be driven from the pasture, the garden had to be weeded, there was wood to be cut and water to be carried." The Eisenhower truck garden in Abilene (three or four acres) presented similar difficulties.

Even more important than the candidate's farm origins, judging by the emphasis given by the biographies, and much more difficult to establish is the candidate's more recent connection with the soil. Ideally, the nomination should find him seated beneath his fig and vine so that the Cincinnatus image may be applied more literally. This has been made at least tenable by the long-standing practice of successful Americans, with or without farm backgrounds, of buying and operating a farm after making their fortunes in the city. Thus it becomes possible for the campaign biographer to take lyric delight in fashioning such romantic pastoral evocations as this one: "Horatio Seymour, although a man of the most brilliant parts—a profound scholar, a magnificent orator, a wise, sagacious and experienced statesman—is only a plain farmer after all. From the peaceful and pleasant occupations of rural life, he has been called by the unanimous voice of the great party of the people to become their standard-bearer . . . he stands before the nation to-day as the proudest specimen of American yeomanry the world has ever looked upon. In the quiet retirement of his country home, he has, while earnestly devoting himself to the tilling of the soil, been giving the best energies of his comprehensive mind to national affairs." And, of course, it is with great reluctance that the candidate is persuaded to leave the plow in the furrow: "Like Cincinnatus the Roman statesman, Hayes preferred his fields of wheat, his droves of cattle and swine, to the loftiest and easiest position which the nation could bestow, and left them only when there was an unmistakable need for him in the councils of state."

That entirely superfluous committee which calls on a candidate to announce to him that he has received the nomination might have found Greeley doing the chores, Garfield "working in the hay-field with his boys," Bryan "nursing an ailing pig back to health," Cox "happy . . . amongst the animals," Willkie tramping over his acres, or even the urbane Mr. Dewey among his cabbages at Pawling.[1]

One and all, they are almost literally dragged from their rural retreats. The nobility and self-sacrificing patriotism that prompts the candidate to abandon the "sweets of rural occupation" to save the state is, of course, powerfully reinforced by the example of Washington—in Lord Byron's phrase: "The first, the best, the Cincinnatus of the West." And their biographers do not fail to point out the remarkable coincidence that their candidates, *too* have found real happiness only amid the pursuits of husbandry.

The Cincinnatus image is, of course, only the vehicle, a sort of cultural cliché, through which the appeal is made to a deeply rooted group of ideas concerning the values inherent in agrarian pursuits. Since campaign biographies, quite naturally, are neither subtle nor

[1] There is a certain amount of self-consciousness in some of these recent biographies; thus Walker says in his campaign life of Dewey: "He makes no pretense, however, of being an authentic dirt farmer; he has never even had his picture taken running a tractor or pitching hay, although the temptation might have been strong." (This same biography, incidentally, includes a picture of Dewey as a farm boy in overalls, one of him sitting on a rail fence talking with the old farmer for whom he worked as a boy, and one of him and his children among the cabbages at Pawling.)

learned, these values are also spelled out. There is, for example, a constant statement of the time-honored belief that agriculture is "the greatest source of national wealth and happiness." References are made to the Jeffersonian faith in the yeomanry as the backbone of political democracy—"that useful class, which has since given the spring to the glory and prosperity of the state." They form an anchor of stability for the nation. "They are," said a biographer of Buchanan, "the body of men, among whom you may expect to find in an eminent degree that virtue without which your American institutions could not continue to exist." For, living in rural isolation, away from the teeming hustle of cities, "men think. They take time to think." Truman was quoted by his biographer on this point: "Riding one of those plows all day, day after day, gives one time to think. I've settled all the ills of mankind in one way or another riding along, seeing that each animal pulled his part of the load." And the simplicity of the agrarian life is more in keeping with the Spartan virtue of the early Republic "than commerce, which builds up luxury, and fosters aristocratic classes." And, of course, as one approaches the present, the memory of the Golden Age of the Republic grows mellower and the usual sigh for the "good old days" is heard: "Judge Parker is a product of that plain, faithful, toilsome, frugal, substantial country life of old, examples of which have grown so rare that they are now to be specially remarked."

While it is, of course, obvious to biographers that the pursuits of husbandry provide the candidate with physical health and vigor, this is but a minor consideration. Of much greater import is their acceptance of the almost mystical idea that this proximity to nature engenders a sort of moral or spiritual health. "The best elements of our American life have always come up from the hardy, vigorous stratum that was nearest to the soil and in some ways dependent on it." It is productive of unfogged intelligence: "From the healthy surroundings and disciplines of pastoral pursuits may emerge the most vigorous and brilliant minds. . . ."

In short, it is not only natural but highly desirable that, as one campaign biographer put it, "Our bare-footed plough-boys rise to ride the Steed of State, and wield the rod of republican empire." Their preparation has been in the best tradition of Cincinnatus, Cromwell, and Washington. Can it be doubted, asked a biographer of Coolidge in 1924, that "such cumulative experience in meeting and overcoming all the farmer's problems is sufficient to develop capacity for statesmanship."

These astute political propagandists have had ample reason to believe that there will be few doubters, for the universal esteem that has been traditionally accorded the pursuits of the agricultural life is very old. Hesiod, Aristotle, Xenophon, Cato, Cicero, Horace, and Virgil, to mention but a few, extolled the virtues of a life devoted to the tilling of the soil. In this agrarian mystique, firmly established in Western culture at latest by the time of Augustus, virtue radiated up through the plow handles, infusing the plowman with honor, manliness, noble thought, patriotism, civic responsibility, and all the immemorial virtues. It persisted through the Middle Ages, gathering strength from scriptural sanction and from other Christian sources, and bloomed mightily in the Renaissance with the revival of classical learning. After a brief waning in the sixteenth and seventeenth centuries, the praise of husbandry burst forth with tremendous new vigor in the eighteenth century, replete with intensified mystical and romantic overtones.

Exploring the persistent phenomenon, A. Whitney Griswold has offered a simple "common-sense" explanation: "Much of this writing, all of it perhaps, was an idealization of the circumstances in which men had lived and labored throughout most of their history. For thousands of years agriculture had been the principal means of livelihood. Even today it employs two-thirds of the human race. Only for a brief moment in history and in a few places on earth have men known anything but an agrarian environment. Since agriculture was the basic economic enterprise, the traditional calling of mankind, it is not surprising to find it sanctioned by religion, by secular idealism, by whatever forms in which the human propensity for rationalization found expression. Almost all men were farmers, therefore to think well of man was to think well of farming."

This ancient tradition, then, came to America as a part of the "cultural baggage" of the settlers. Transplanted in the virgin soil of the New World it throve mightily. The immensity of the new land area offered seemingly limitless opportunity for agriculturists, and from the very beginning the promotional literature boosting settlement fairly wallows in all the old, extravagant praise of the land and the agrarian life. With the coming of the Revolution a new element of belief enters the agrarian creed. This new article of faith asserted that the farmer was the backbone of political democracy. Briefly, the rationale of the belief rests upon the assumption that democracy requires free men capable of making free decisions. This condition would obtain in America as long as there remained an abundance of land, making it relatively easy for men to acquire a freehold, because possession of a freehold meant economic independence and, in turn, political independence.

This attribute of the sturdy yeoman rapidly rose to a position of prominence in the agrarian mythology. Exploring this theme in early American literature, Chester E. Eisinger concludes: "The archetypal American—the rugged, individualistic, self-sustaining, independent farmer—thus becomes the object of a chorus of chauvinistic praise. This figure sent shivers of ecstasy up and down the spines of his articulate countrymen, the famous and the unknown alike."

Few among the yeoman's admirers could have been more ardent than Thomas Jefferson. As Griswold has pointed out: "No one believed so implicitly as he in a causal connection between the occupation of farming and the political system of democracy, and no one, before or since his time, has given that belief a greater impetus among his countrymen." It would serve no useful purpose to present the many choice quotations from Jefferson lavishing praise on the yeomanry—this has been done, with monotonous regularity, by the agrarian devotees of their patron saint. It is also a sterile thing to badger the oft-repeated points that Jefferson amended this view: that he was no doctrinaire; that, having lived long and written much, the corpus of his work contains many contradictions —the fact remains that in the mind of the public he has enduringly remained the foremost exemplar of agrarian democracy.

This complex of ideas that clusters around the image of the sturdy yeoman has had a remarkable vitality in America. The existence of the vast area of virgin land that beckoned the American ever westward through most of our history provided opportunity for the continuous renewal of the agrarian tradition. And, like

Antaeus, it gathered strength with each new contact with the earth. Each successive agricultural frontier became in turn the "garden of the world," in the American imagination, and was destined to produce a race of cultivators vigorous of mind, healthy of body, and virtuous in character, who would provide the moral patriotic fiber for the backbone of the nation. The progress of the agrarian myth across the continent, from its beginnings in America up to the close of the frontier, has been traced by Henry Nash Smith in *Virgin Land,* one of the most perceptive studies in American intellectual history yet to appear.

The myth did not die with the passing of the frontier. Six years after the census of 1920 revealed that 51 per cent of the population were urban dwellers, a National Industrial Conference Board declared: "Our farmers are more than a class of our population. Farming is more than an industry. The significance of agriculture in the life of the nation is far deeper than this. It touches something vital and fundamental in the national existence. It involves the national security, the racial character, the economic welfare and the social progress of our people." This same board, together with the National Chamber of Commerce, appointed a Business Men's Commission on Agriculture, made up of prominent railroad executives, bankers, and manufacturers—a most unagrarian group. The following year this commission issued a report that spoke of farming as not just a business but a way of life and the farmer as possessed of "a proud heritage, last bulwark of true democracy." [2]

Surveying the current status of the farm vote on the eve of the presidential election of 1956, one of the leading historians of the role of the farmer in American life concluded: "Despite what has been said . . . farm political power is much stronger than the ratio of farmers to the total population would seem to warrant. . . . Furthermore, there is still a very strong feeling of agricultural fundamentalism in this country, even among city dwellers who would not think of living or working on a farm. The idea that farming

[2] The commission uses some surprisingly Jeffersonian language in its plea for the preservation of the "proud role of the independent proprietor." It even brings in the notion of the farm as the citadel of virtue in contrast to "the temptation of ease and amusement, worst enemies of urban life." *The Condition of Agriculture in the United States and Measures for Its Improvement* (New York and Washington, 1927), 17, 18.

is somehow more pure and virtuous than other occupations and that farmers are God's chosen people is widely believed today as well as in the days of Jefferson." [3]

There is, then, ample evidence that the praises of husbandry found in the campaign biographies echo deeply ingrained ideas that have existed in America from the beginning. Moreover, the belief that farming as a way of life in some mysterious fashion implants in men's characters stability, morality, responsibility, patriotic devotion, and all the sturdy, simple, republican virtues has not been limited to the agricultural population but has had wide currency. It is hardly surprising to find that political propagandists from 1824 to 1960 have not neglected to identify their candidates with this rich lode of precious belief.

[3] Gilbert Fite, "Changing Political Role of the Farmer," *Current History* (August, 1956), 89.

8

FROM THE LAW TO THE
MARKET PLACE

IT IS UNFORTUNATE THAT THE ANCIENT CINCINNATUS DID
not take to the law to supplement his income. For although circumstances often conspired to enable the candidate to tread the boards
for one brief act in the role of idyllic husbandman, ultimately it
becomes necessary for the campaign biographer to face up to the
prosaic fact that his hero really made his living at the law. Two
thirds of all the major party candidates since 1824 have, for at
least part of their careers, practiced law.

The affinity between the legal profession and politics is not, of
course, surprising. "Scarcely a lawyer," wrote the anonymous biographer of Cass, "who is not an aspirant for political distinction,
exists within the United States." Forty years later Lew Wallace
observed that, unlike Ben Harrison, "multitudes of young men
in our country drift toward the law not from any manifest aptitude
for it, but because it has been . . . the directest path to political
prizes."

But since this is obviously not very high ground upon which
to discuss the hero's profession as a preparation for statecraft,
these observations are not lingered over. There are matters enough
to be attended to. Most importantly the profession itself must be
rehabilitated. For, justifiably or not, the biographers are conscious
of the ancient prejudices against the lawyer and make stout efforts
to combat them. Hence, the reader was assured, for example, that
Hayes "showed the surprised people that a lawyer could be a
Christian gentleman and a practical philanthropist." Judging from
the emphasis placed upon it, lawyers demonstrated that they were
"Christian gentlemen" by never appearing in a cause which they
believed to be unjust. Thus Clay "could never be prevailed on, by
offers from the great and affluent, to conduct an unjust or oppres-

sive prosecution. . . ." Lincoln "was never known to undertake a cause which he believed founded in wrong and injustice." Tilden required that his client have "not only the merits in law, but the equity on his side." The candidate acquired a reputation as a "practical philanthropist" during his legal practice by his unhesitating assumption of the causes of poor men, penniless widows, orphans, and the downtrodden in general, without a thought to the fee. (One had to select "downtrodden" clients with some care, however. John W. Davis' biographer felt it necessary to expend four pages of detail exonerating his subject from the charge that he had once defended Eugene V. Debs and Mother Jones.) For those who could pay, his fees were modest. "The small fees which he [Coolidge] charged for legal services were a by-word." Some even rose to the supreme virtue of discouraging litigation. Hayes "was one of those lawyers, not at all so rare as the general fame of the profession would imply, who discourage litigation in their clients."

Although from the foregoing one might easily leap to the conclusion that the candidates experienced indifferent financial success in the practice of their professions, such was not the case. Indeed, all were eminently successful, and success at the bar, as in the other professions followed by the candidates, is measured in monetary terms. "Success attended his [Jackson's] industry and talents; he acquired a lucrative business in the courts. . . ." Characteristically, this success stops short of wealth. "Avarice being no trait in Mr. Buchanan's character, he gladly sought repose from business, when Providence had blessed his labors with the realization of the sincere prayer of Agar, 'give me neither poverty nor riches.'" Coolidge "had New England thrift deeply embedded in his mind; but beyond the supply of the simple necessaries of life for his modest household, money-making was evidently a matter that made little or no appeal to him." This commendable lack of greed should not be confused with a lack of ambition. Ambition is directed toward more salutary goals. "By the profits of a legal practice [Clay] . . . could now afford . . . to devote his time to the service of this country." The candidates could, if they chose, have gone on to the acquisition of great wealth, for they possessed the talent and the industry. "Had he [Blaine] chosen a business life, his wealth would have equaled that of a Vanderbilt."

94

Thus, despite the heavy emphasis placed upon success and the invariable interpretation of success in terms of financial gain, it would be unjust and inaccurate to present this achievement of the candidate as adequate in itself as a preparation for statecraft. Nowhere in the whole series of biographies can one find, even implicitly, the bald proposition that the possession of wealth is a requisite or even a recommendation for an aspirant to the presidential office.

Financial success is rather the outward badge that designates the wearer as the possessor of certain qualities that are of solid worth in the practice of statecraft. In short, the candidate is here cast in the role of that uniquely American folk hero, the successful *businessman*. Whether his business career has come by way of the law or any other avenue, he has learned the value of a dollar, has handled large enterprise with prudence and caution, has acquired the habit of efficiency, and has achieved the reputation of being "safe and sound."

As early as 1824 the candidate (General Jackson) was being praised for "preserving system in his monied transactions," for his "marked punctuality" in business affairs, and for regulating "properly his *balance of trade*." Knowledge of the value of a dollar, the ability to "guard a dollar well and compel it to perform its proper purpose" was not only a characteristic of Bryan but is a universal trait among candidates. The self-made men among the candidates do not enjoy a monopoly of this trait; it is found in professional soldier candidates like Hancock and candidates born to wealth like Stevenson. "He [Stevenson] always worries a great deal about money—his own, the State's, anybody's."

The magnitude of the business enterprise that has enjoyed the benefits of the candidate's talents is not always as apparent as in the case of Willkie, whose biographer could write happily about his hero boosting sales from "$5,000,000 to more than $20,000,-000 per year." Taft's biographer, for example, found it necessary to explain just how his judicial duties and other governmental posts involved him in "tremendous business undertakings." To disabuse the voter-reader of the notion that a university president was little more than a glorified school teacher called forth similar labors on the part of the biographers of Wilson. "The position of

95

college president in modern times," wrote one of them with colossal understatement, "has called for more executive ability than what is termed scholarship."

Efficiency is a matter of bringing to one's work habits of orderliness, thus eliminating wasted time and motion. Systemization reached its apotheosis in Hoover—"the human symbol of efficiency." But for a considerable period before the advent of the Great Engineer, candidates were demonstrating that they had learned these lessons well by applying "business methods" to the conduct of their affairs. An interesting comparison that suggests the long continuity of the qualities that make up the businessman folk hero are these two quotations from campaign biographies separated by nearly fifty years: "Mr. Tilden's success in rescuing corporations from unprofitable and embarrassing litigation, in reorganizing their administration, in reëstablishing their credit, and in rendering their resources available, soon gave him an amount of business which was limited only by his physical ability to conduct it." In 1928 it was written of Hoover: "He was toward the end a great doctor of sick companies. When a concern which ought to produce and pay did not produce or pay, after every one else gave up they called in Hoover. He diagnosed the trouble and cured it."

The habits and skills acquired during this vast experience have earned for the candidate a solid reputation among his peers. Businessmen regard him as "sound." The biographer of Tilden asserted, reassuringly, that "His counsel has been sought for twenty years by the safe and conservative capitalists of the country, and not by the stock-jobbers and reckless speculators, for with them he refused to have any dealings." This sort of assurance runs throughout the biographies; only the modifying adjective varies: Jackson was a "sagacious" businessman; Pierce was "safe"; Cleveland was "careful"; Cox was "conservative"; Landon was "sound."

While it is true that every stage of the candidate's life becomes, in the facile hands of the campaign biographer, but a step in the preparation of the man for his hour, the private pursuits whereby he made his living as an adult have a certain immediacy not encountered before. This is the "jumping off point" for a career in public life, the apprenticeship for statecraft. The qualities, habits, and skills acquired during this apprenticeship have a direct application to the "job" to which he aspires.

This immediacy is less true for the attempts to cast the candidate in the role of Cincinnatus called from the plow to save the state. The treatment of the candidate's farming career is as idealized as any of the qualities previously discussed and, like them, it identifies the candidate with a horde of precious beliefs. As the candidate's connection with the soil grows increasingly tenuous, the treatment of this aspect of his career grows more nostalgic and unreal, but there is no real sign that the beliefs that occasion it are being discarded.

Idealization continues to dominate in the treatment of the candidate as a lawyer—presenting him as an unselfish handmaiden of justice and champion of the oppressed—but it rapidly dissipates as the candidate's legal career shades into the role of successful businessman. The biographer here tends to treat his subject as a *real* businessman in contrast to his previous treatment of him as an *ideal* farmer, soldier, and youth. It is apparent that the biographers feel that the application of the virtues that have spelled success for the candidate in business—great executive ability embodying financial wisdom, caution and responsibility, efficiency and practicality—is direct and immediate. They belong not to the hero's past but to his present. They are not qualities from which a desirable course of conduct as chief executive can reasonably be expected to spring; they are themselves a course of conduct that merely require a transference of their application from private business to the public business. But because the attributes that make up the role of successful businessman are of a specific, direct, and tangible nature, it should not be inferred that they are any the less regarded as ideals.

Basically, there is little discernible evolution in the role of the candidate as successful lawyer-businessman. In general, his period of law practice becomes increasingly brief as we approach the present and the treatment of this phase becomes correspondingly less detailed. And, as one might expect, the magnitude of the business enterprise that he engages in receives an increasing amount of attention.

In undertaking an exploration of the cultural ideas appealed to in the biographers' treatment of the adult private careers of the candidates, it should be made clear at the outset that the qualities allegedly produced by each of these professions—farmer, lawyer, and businessman—are intended to have a universal appeal. The qualities singled out for praise are of such a general and endearing nature that it is patent that the biographers believed that all hearts and minds, regardless of occupation, would be touched by each of them.

In regard to the qualities that allegedly are nurtured by the pursuit of agriculture, this belief in a universal appeal was well founded. Turning from farming to the law, quite a different situation is encountered. In presenting the legal career of the candidate, the biographer is on the defensive. The burden of proof has shifted. The biographer must demonstrate that his subject has remained virtuous *despite* his profession.

In his realization that he must anticipate hostility on the part of his voter-reader the biographer again demonstrates his sound understanding of his audience. For if the good opinion of farmers is very old, there is an equally ancient bad opinion of lawyers. "In all centuries in which they have existed," writes William Seagle, "lawyers have been unpopular with the common people." The England from which the early colonists came took a decidedly unfavorable view of the legal profession. Some idea of the lawyer's reputation among his neighbors can be gathered from the titles of the numerous tracts being hawked in seventeenth-century London: *The Downfall of Unjust Lawyers; Doomsday Drawing Near with Thunder and Lightning for Lawyers; A Rod for Lawyers Who are Hereby Declared Robbers and Deceivers of the Nation.*

This prejudice came with the colonists to the New World. "Nothing," says Charles Warren, "in the early legal history of the Colonies is more striking than the uniformly low position held in the community by the members of the legal profession, and the slight part which they played in the development of the country until nearly the middle of the Eighteenth Century. In every one of the Colonies, practically throughout the Seventeenth Century, a lawyer or attorney was a character of disrepute and of suspicion. . . ."

The usual view is that the coming of the Revolutionary crisis catapulted the lawyer out of his despised position into national prominence and esteem. He became the chief spokesman for his countrymen in their quarrels with the Crown after mid-century and took the lead in all of the important councils during the Revolution. It is pointed out, for example, that the proportion of delegates who were lawyers in the Congress that adopted the Declaration of Independence and the Convention that framed the Constitution was very high; that Patrick Henry, Thomas Jefferson, George Wythe, and James Madison were professionally-trained lawyers.

Then, according to the leading authorities, an amazing thing happens: "Nothing in legal history is more curious than the sudden revival, after the War of the Revolution, of the old dislike and distrust of lawyers as a class. For a time, it seemed as if their great services had been forgotten and as if their presence was to be deemed an injury to the Nation." This new wave of hatred for the profession reached its climax in Massachusetts in 1786 when Shays's Rebellion vented pent-up violence on lawyers and courts.

More recently, scholars have not been inclined to accept these precipitous ups and downs of popular esteem. Their research reveals that the prejudice did not vanish during the Revolution suddenly to reappear afterwards. The prejudice remained constant, then as now, but accompanying it was a steady growth in prestige marked by the growth of professional legal training, the maturing of the judicial system, and the entrance into the profession of capable men of unquestionable integrity. Thus James Willard Hurst concludes: "From colonial days popular attitudes conceded to the bar a marked measure of honorable distinction. Yet this was always matched in popular lore by a character for sharpness, pettifogging, and greedy manipulation of technicality to oppress the weak and ignorant." Regardless of this ambivalence in the popular mind, there is ample evidence that the law was believed the surest route to political preferment as early as the mid-eighteenth century and remained so until the twentieth.

With a recognition of this continuously divided state of mind, it becomes easier to understand the late persistence of the campaign biographer's concern to defend the candidate's career as a lawyer. In the nineteenth century the law may well have been "second only to the role of captain of industry as the road to success for the poor boy of the Horatio Alger legend." It may have been, as Alexis de Tocqueville noted in the 1830's and Lord Bryce at the end of the century, the path to political honors and social prestige. But throughout the century the stock villain of the melo-drama remained that "forecloser of mortgages and pursuer of maidens"—the lawyer.

Certainly it is true that the legal profession stands in far greater repute today than it did in the seventeenth and eighteenth centuries. But to assume that the ancient prejudice has worked itself out of the systems of Americans would be inaccurate. Very recently the American Bar Association has been engaged in a monumental study of the legal profession. Hundreds of investigators have been com-piling thousand of pages of reports on every aspect of the lawyer's work. Among the problems this "Survey of the Legal Profession" grappled with was the status of the profession in American society. The survey discovered that whereas the eighteenth century could sum up its opinion in Poor Richard's six well-chosen words, "A good lawyer, a bad neighbor," the twentieth was merely more wordy. Thus Carl Sandburg wrote:

> Why is there a secret singing
> When a lawyer cashes in?
> Why does the hearse horse snicker
> Hauling a lawyer away?

"And so it goes," the survey concludes, "whether in prose or poetry, over the radio or on television, in the movies or in just plain con-versation, the lawyer is the convenient butt for the jokester, the target for the wit, and the villain prototype for the writer of scripts and scenarios. And there are even those who would agree with the Shakespearean character (in *II Henry IV*) who suggested, 'The first thing we do let's kill all the lawyers.' " The surveyors felt it their mournful duty to report to the brotherhood of the bar that although economically, politically, and even socially they are quite well off, as a group they are "surprisingly unpopular."

It has been suggested that this divided state of mind that allows the lawyer to gain political, economic, and social prestige in a so-ciety that does not wholly trust him is at least in part due to the mystery that has long surrounded the common law and the ritual of courts. This mystery is wholly lacking in the pursuits of the businessman. Coolidge's summary may lack appeal to the liberal imagination but it has the virtue of accuracy—"the business of America *is* business."

There is no need to reiterate here the long tradition behind the exaltation of the middle-class virtues of thrift, hard work, orderliness and patient prudence in America. The essentials have been examined in Chapter V in the discussion of the cult of success. The concern here is with the poor boy *after* he has made good. More particularly, the focus is upon the qualities that enabled him to make good and, most crucial of all, the idea that these qualities are not only admirable but necessary for the conduct of the first office of the state. To feel a necessity to explain why orderliness, efficiency, economy, prudence, and caution—in short, "good business methods"—are essential virtues would seem the height of absurdity to Americans. Nothing could be more patent; it is a basic assumption of what one historian has called "Our Business Civilization." Setting out to discuss the *mythos* of American society and the place of the businessman in the "hierarchy of divinities," Thurman Arnold sagely observes that "this hierarchy is never recognized as a mythology during the period when it is most potent. It is only the myths of other peoples or other times that we label as myths." In this mythology, Arnold continues, "The predominant figure was the American Businessman. Warriors were respected but they had a distinctly minor place. The National Government had to imitate the American Businessman. Whenever it failed, people became alarmed."

It is only when the American businessman is viewed in broad historical perspective and in comparison with his counterparts in other nations that the full import of his unique esteem emerges. He has come to occupy this position through a combination of historic and economic factors. The circumstances surrounding the beginning of the nation eliminated his competitors for the chief place in the national pantheon. Peopled by middle-class, dissenting English Protestants for the most part, the nation eliminated any traces of a lingering affection for his rivals—aristocrat, warrior, and princely churchman—in the Revolution. The egalitarian spirit released by the Revolution was nurtured by conditions of life in America. A fixed hostility to the threefold instruments of tyranny —hereditary privilege, standing armies, and a state church—became part of the national creed. Freed from interference by and competition with their traditional rivals and provided with a virgin continent to exploit, the American businessman and the yeoman farmer went on to build a nation and to enjoy, uncontested, the esteem of their countrymen. With the breakup of agrarian power after the Civil War, the last rival of the businessman was eliminated. His virtues became, in the nation's eyes, the qualities that in a few short years transformed a wilderness into the most powerful nation on earth, whose citizens dwell in utopian abundance.

To remind the nation of its continuing debt of gratitude and to suggest to it the absurdity of flirting with heresies that mock at the tried and true canons of sound business methods, the National Federation of Independent Business periodically counts America's blessings: "Let us all Think American. Let us all Talk American. Let us all Do Business the American Way. No nation on earth regardless of its form of government, ever gave to human beings so much liberty and material prosperity as our own Constitutional form of Freedom. We started out as thirteen little States, ridden by poverty and threatened by savages. We were, however, blessed by God. We now represent the utmost in individual freedom and individual prosperity. Compare our United States with any other land on earth. The workingman here is a king compared to the workingman in any other country. Nearly all of us have modern homes —electric lights and power—gas cooking—telephones—automobiles —automatic refrigeration—electric washers and irons—radios— insurance policies. Most of us own bonds and have money in the bank, plus a thousand and one other conveniences and luxuries. Are we ready to exchange all this for the crazy promises of some foreign crackpot?"

In the year 1953 two spokesmen representing very different types of business agreed that Americans owe loyalty to the American businessman and to the qualities that have spelled success not only for this businessman himself but also for his country. One of them announced with simple sincerity that what was good for General Motors was good for the country. The other, assistant to the Chairman of the Conference of American Small Business Organizations, wrote: "Our loyalty is not a selfish loyalty to the little businessman—it is rather a loyalty to the America that he, and millions who preceded him, built."

The several occupations that combine so readily in the career of the candidate, each adding their distinctive contributions to the formation of a citizen eminently prepared for executive leadership, do not present the same harmonious co-existence in the life of the nation from which they are drawn. Farmers have consistently believed that businessmen were their natural enemies, the source of all their woes; businessmen in turn have regarded farmers as the chief source of inflationary heresies and a perpetual peril to a sound economy; both have turned a fine scorn on the lawyer who, in their view, thriving on other people's troubles, seems to win no matter whose side he may be on. In short, farmers, lawyers, and businessmen, paired in one combination or another, have opposed each other in nearly every period of American history. And this antithesis could be extended to include not only what they have believed to be their economic and political interests but also their ideas, attitudes, and the qualities and virtues they have claimed as the peculiar attributes that emanated from a life devoted to their particular occupations. Thus, for example, rather than seeing the farmer as the sturdy yeoman, the urban elements (including businessman and lawyer) had come, at latest by the 1870's, to see him as Cousin Reuben with hayseed in his hair, come to gawk at the tall buildings. The farmer, in turn, did not often dwell upon the businessman's efficiency and managerial ability but consistently regarded him as a parasite who lived upon the cultivator's labor. To him it was absurd to expect virtue in lawyers and businessmen, who resided amidst all the ultimate in wickedness in the Sodoms and Gomorrahs of America.

That it avoids the hazards presented by this other side of the coin illustrates how marvelously uncomplicated is the life of the campaign biography. The prescription for combining in one man three mutually antagonistic occupations is delightfully simple: merely abstain from recording what the subject thought about each of the other two roles while he enacted the third, and present only those ideas attached to the various occupations that will antagonize no one.

Thus is the candidate made ready to face the tasks of statecraft, anointed successively with the peculiar virtues of three of the major occupations of his countrymen.

9

STATESMAN, OR THE POLITICIAN TRANSFIGURED

THE PRECEDING CHAPTERS HAVE BROUGHT THE CANDIDATE to the threshold of his career in public life. From his ancestry to his adult occupation, each phase of his history has been pregnant with meaning for the future. All events have conspired to produce in him a superb ripeness for the tasks of statesmanship. It is of the utmost importance to observe that his preparation is now complete, in spite of the fact that no mention has been made of his experience in public office. It is perhaps an extremely hazardous generalization to put forward, but one that seems justified by the evidence, that an apprenticeship in politics is, in the view of the campaign biographer, a liability. The feeling is inescapable that the biographers turn to the political careers of their subjects with great reluctance—something akin to the feeling of a mother who has carefully and immaculately groomed her young son and then released him to romp with his unwashed playmates.

Certainly one would expect, and one does find, that the biographers make the best of a bad situation. There are obvious assets to be found in state and national careers as administrators or legislators. But the great unresolved problem is whether this undeniably valuable experience is worth the risk of contamination that it entails. The contamination is spread by the virus politics. Because most candidates have had a career in political life before their nomination, inescapably the admission must be made that the biographer's hero is a politician. Apparently the word "politician" was not freighted with derogatory implications before 1840. The anonymous biographer of John Quincy Adams felt called upon to defend his subject against the charge "that he [was] *not* fitted for a practical politician." "This," he continued, "*if well founded,* would of itself have sufficed to exclude Mr. Adams from all consideration, as a candidate for the

Presidency." In a similar vein the biographers of Jackson, Clay, and Van Buren discoursed unabashedly on their talents as politicians.

It is difficult to fix the date when the term "politician" begins to take on a sinister character. This usage does, however, definitely occur in one of the biographies of William Henry Harrison in 1840. By 1844 there can be little doubt that henceforth to use the word without some qualifying adjective was to damn utterly. In that year a biographer of Clay denounced the enemies of Harry of the West as "politicians by trade [who] look to the success of party for living. Not a few of them are loafers and spongers—with nothing to loose [*sic*] and everything to gain. By politics they make their meat and bread—by politics they live and move and have their being—and at their trade they work!" Here is the heart of the matter—a politician is an evil thing when he is a "politician by trade."

From 1844 onward whenever it is an unavoidable fact that a candidate has been a politician, great care is taken to assure the voter-reader that he has never been a "mere politician." He may, like Buchanan, have been a student of "the science of political economy"; or, like Hayes, he may have mastered the "study of politics—which is but another name for contemporary history"; or frequently he may be called, like Garfield, "a politician in the larger and better sense." But above all, he is never a *professional* politician. Cleveland, the reader was assured, "knows little of the machinery of conducting close campaigns"; Hancock "never mingled in political cabals"; and Hayes "always refused to be a professional politician." Perhaps the most succinct statement of this theme was achieved by the biographer of John W. Davis, who quoted Davis' old family physician: " 'John don't know a damn thing about politics and never did.' "

The role of amateur in politics is one dearly beloved of campaign biographers. The amateur's openhanded, unselfish devotion to the cause of good government stands in splendid contrast to the sordid machinations of professionals. The amateur is at his finest in the scenes in which he confounds the "schemes of the politicians." "The professional politicians were a good deal astonished as the canvass, preceding the convention, advanced," the biographer of Tilden gloated back in 1876. In 1936 Landon's biographer took the same sort of pleasure in reporting that "The smart politicians sat back with that peculiar look of men who have seen water flow upstream and said, 'I swan.' " Before he lost his amateur standing by accepting the support of Colonel Jacob Arvey and his Cook County machine, "Stevenson's campaign looked like something run by the Rover Boys."

The amateur in politics has taken a new twist in the twentieth century. Between 1840 and 1900, if it was not necessary to distinguish their candidate as a politician "in the better sense of the word" or to insist upon his amateur standing, the biographer was delighted and more than willing to let the matter rest with the rather emphatic statement that the candidate was *not* a politician. This was the case for biographers of William Henry Harrison, Taylor, Scott, McClellan, Grant, and Hancock. But beginning with Wilson candidates with little or no political experience, like Hoover and Willkie, are presented as endowed with a sort of native political wisdom that manifests itself as soon as their hats land in the ring. "It was," boasted a biographer of Wilson in 1912, "indeed, a tremendous surprise to the shrewd politicians to find on board the ship of state a skilful and efficient political captain, who understood the most direct course, who read the compass with perfect accuracy, and who saw each flashlight and signal in time to avoid the breakers and shoals. It was true that the new commander had never before held a captain's license. He had never even been a first mate in the game of politics." Concerning the Great Engineer as Secretary of Commerce, the reader was told that "It was at one time the fashion on Capitol Hill to remark that Hoover was no politician. But since some of our elected representatives noticed that above all other members of the cabinet he gets his appropriations through, we have heard less of that!" And no one, it develops, need worry about "the Abraham Lincoln of Wall Street": "Willkie is no Johnny-Come-Lately to the strange science and art of politics. Politics come as naturally to him as hitting home runs did to Babe Ruth."

It is just as important to defend the candidate against the charge that he is a "blind partisan" as it is to defend him against an indictment as a "mere politician." Politicians are placemen; placemen come to power through the instrument of party. Indeed, a blind adherence to party finds condemnation in the campaign biographies from the very beginning.

Just as there was, necessarily, no wholesale condemnation of politicians but, rather, a separation of the amateur from the professional, so there is no blanket indictment of political parties or of the candidate's attachment to a party. There are, throughout, repeated assertions of the idea that a political party represents a set of political beliefs—a sort of creed—and there is no hesitation in admitting the candidate's profession of faith. As a matter of fact, it has proved useful as a sort of shorthand device to "explain" the candidate's political ideas by phrases like "he has steadily adhered to the political maxims of that school [the Republican party]." On rare occasions a case will be made for the political party as essential to the proper functioning of the government. Impatient with the hypocrisy of politicians who obscured this important fact, an anonymous biographer wrote of Polk: "It is true that despising the cant of *no party*, which has ever been the pretext of selfish and treacherous politicians, and convinced that in a popular government nothing can be accomplished by isolated action, he has always acted with his party, as far as principle would justify." In a similar vein Cleveland defended the party as "an open and sturdy partnership" which, when properly conducted, serves the ends of the people efficiently.

Since, then, it is safe to claim an attachment to party within the limits discussed above, it is not uncommon to find biographers claiming for their subjects a lifelong affiliation. Hancock was "born a Democrat. . . ." Only slightly less precocious, Polk was "From his early youth . . . a Republican of the 'straightest set.'" Hoover and Eisenhower "had been brought up Republicans." In a young party, like the Republican party, some come to be almost charter members. Thus it was claimed (incorrectly, of course) that Lincoln was one of the first to join the Republican party in Illinois; Hayes was an organizer in Ohio; Garfield worked for Frémont in 1856; and Dewey's grandfather was a delegate to the Jackson, Michigan, convention of 1854.

That which is most condemned in party politics is the sort of regularity that sacrifices principle and country for the sake of party advantage and that functions through intrigue and machine politics. Ideally, a candidate should behave like John Quincy Adams, of whom it was claimed: "It was not enough for him, that a proposition, affecting any great national interest, originated with *this* or *that party*, to secure it to his support: He examined it on the broad ground of *principle*, and opposed or defended it, according to the honest dictates of a judgement unshackled by preconceptions." But although all insist that in the consideration of measures their hero

107

places principle above party, not many approve so austere a course. Generally speaking, party regularity is expected and principle comes into play only where there is a question of sacrificing one or the other. The biographer of Theodore Roosevelt put it as well as any: "He might indeed quarrel with the party of a lifetime, for he would as little surrender his conscience to a multitude of men as to one, and he has said that he does not number party loyalty with the ten commandments, firmly as he holds to it to get things done." The exact nature of the principle or principles that must occasionally be defended against the demands of party regularity are almost never made explicit. Gestures in this direction simply amount to equating principle with equally vague generalities like truth, justice, and the welfare of the people.

There is another aspect of the collision between the claims of party and the dictates of principle. Here the candidate is faced with a choice of men rather than measures. No ambiguities cloud the meaning of principle here. The candidate has the alternative of rewarding his friends and punishing his enemies or choosing officeholders on the basis of merit. Obviously, no one would freely undertake the role of spoilsman. From first to last the biographies teem with assurances that no one need fear that the new broom will sweep clean. In 1824 the citizenry were promised that Jackson was "not . . . one of those blind infatuated partizans, who holds the opinions of others in derision, and determines the good or bad qualities of a man, according as he belongs to this or the other political sect; but influenced by higher and nobler sentiments, acts on the liberal principle, that

> 'Honour and shame from no condition rise,
> Act well your part, there all the honour lies—
> Worth makes the man, and want of it the fellow.' "

In 1944 the same sort of assurance was echoed by the biographer of Dewey, who offered as proof of this good intention the fact that when Dewey was elected governor of New York "there was, in fact, no general exodus of Democratic office holders. . . . [no] traditional blanket indictment." Over the years this theme has become incorporated into a kind of stereotyped argument that goes like this: this man sought no office; the office sought him; therefore, he owes no obligations to political organizations; his only obligation is to the people; hence, in making appointments to office he will be a free agent, guided only by his duty to the people.

It is always made abundantly clear that the candidate's stand for principle in the choice of men and measures is not merely something that the citizens have a right to expect. This is uncommon purity, not usually met with in the usual run of men in public life. Biographers never weary of pointing out the great risk of personal advantage such a stand entails. Bryan's unhesitating devotion to principle made "his own party friends and managers shudder" for his political future. Wilson was applauded for "his unflinching attachment to principle at a time when calculations of personal expediency would have counseled a different course." And Truman "acted like a man who did not mind risking grave political consequences, who would 'rather be right than be President.'"

This courage to rise above the demands of party not only vindicates the faith of his friends but also secures the approbation and even the support of his political foes. Apart from offering to them a paragon of virtue, this is the most direct attempt to woo the opposition that the biographies make. "Right thinking men" of the opposing party, it is pointed out, have throughout the candidate's political career paid homage to this unselfish ability to rise above partisanship for the sake of the general welfare. Coolidge "never failed, from his first campaign onward, to be supported by a considerable proportion of Democratic votes." This has been true from the time of John Quincy Adams, who "was alternatively claimed by *both* parties" during his early career in the Senate, to the present.

The one remaining aspect of the campaign biographers' treatment of political parties is their indictment of the methods parties employ to secure political victory. This is the institutional counterpart of the distinction between the professional and the amateur in politics. Prior to the 1870's the party methods that were assailed were in general whatever smacked of a violation of fair play—secret deals, irresponsible charges, violent abuse, and intrigue. A biographer of Clay pretty well summed up what was believed to be not cricket: "For the attainment of his present attitude before the American people, Mr. Clay has resorted to no secret management—no low party intrigue. He has circulated none of that poison, visible only in its baneful effects, which modern demagogues have been pouring into the veins of the body politick."

Beginning in the 1870's the biographers come to concentrate their cries of outrage on that aspect of party politics represented by the "boss" and the "machine." In most cases the "boss" has proved to be a very popular dragon. The first to don the armor of St. George was Tilden, who sallied forth to cow Boss Tweed. The intrepid Garfield bagged three bosses *within his own party*—Conkling, Logan, and Cameron, who "like Caesar, Cassius and Pompey [would] divide the empire between them. . . ." Theodore Roosevelt was pictured as "a lusty young David facing the Tammany Goliath."

However, dragons are not always in season. The biographers of Democratic candidates in particular have sometimes had a bad time explaining away their hero's connection with the big city machine. Cleveland's biographers cut the Tammany albatross loose with a clean stroke; so did Wilson's. Of late, however, the bird will not down so easily. In his campaign biography of Al Smith, Franklin Roosevelt, who obviously could not have been expected to disassociate the Big Chief from his Braves, made a gesture by quoting "the head of one of the great non-partisan groups devoted to social and governmental reform" to the effect that " 'that man Smith and the younger crowd with him represent a new spirit in Tammany Hall.' " The biographers of Roosevelt himself had a difficult time with this problem, tossing him from one side of the fence to the other, and winding up by conveying the general impression that for FDR, St. Tammany had been an ugly but occasionally useful servant. Freely acknowledging Stevenson's connection with Colonel Jacob Arvey, his biographer explained that this was not necessarily fatal: "He [Stevenson] says the Cook County organization 'adopted' him. There is truth in this. But it does not mean the machine runs him. In matters that affect him, he runs the machine."

Thus far, this description of the handling of the candidate's political apprenticeship has attempted to emphasize its defensive character. The conclusion is inescapable that the basic assumptions of the biographers are that their audience believes the politician is evil and party politics is evil twice compounded. Their reluctance to conduct the shining knight they have created along the narrow, slippery paths that run through the mire is understandable. This situation, quite naturally, requires that most of the biographer's efforts be bent toward convincing the voter-reader of the things that his candidate is not—he is not this kind of a politician; he is not that kind of a party man.

But dealing in negations is distasteful to the campaign biographer. It is incompatible with the creative process. The joy of fashioning the clay of the candidate's real life into an ideal model is dimmed. It is, then, with something of a triumphant note that he resumes the offensive. Two themes, each thoroughly positive in nature, can be extracted from this otherwise barren desert of negations that forms the candidate's political apprenticeship. So grateful is he for these reinforcements that enable him once again to mount an attack, that he employs them over and over again until they are thoroughly exhausted. Quantitatively, no other specific themes loom so large in campaign biographies as (1) the idea that the office has sought the man and (2) the identification of the candidate with the political heroes of the past.

Since the innumerable instances in which the theme of the office seeks the man occur are all essentially the same, the temptation to present an extensive sampling of the fervid and extravagant language in which they are often couched will have to be resisted. It does seem, however, worth pointing out that the flight from office becomes more headlong as the years go by. Jackson seemed merely coy when "with his characteristic delicacy and sense of propriety, [he] kept aloof from every act that might possibly be construed into an aim toward his own aggrandizement." By 1904 the candidate (T.R.) had come "to thunder against himself. He was no shy and modest objector. He pleaded and stormed." By 1948 "It became almost an obsession with Truman that he never wanted to be President." But regardless of the varying degrees of extravagance of language, the idea is always the same. The candidate, a humble man utterly devoid of ambition, must be dragged into office by a people who will not be denied their right to be ruled by their finest. Painful as it may be, the candidate, after having been drafted, comes to agree reluctantly that this is the people's right. Thus his biographer wrote of Charles Evans Hughes: "He felt that the citizenship of the Nation had the right to summon to the Presidency any man in the land, and that no man had the right to place his own preference for a present post of service above the right of the people to requisition for the Presidency the best ability at their command."

111

It is a melancholy duty to have to record the fact that the cheapening of this splendid ideal of responsible service has gone so far that its abuse is now being pointed out by campaign biographers themselves. "The word draft is almost universally misunderstood," wrote one biographer of Stevenson. "Politicians have used it so often to describe rigged nominations that most people have concluded that a genuine draft never occurs. By and large, this is true. But one did occur in 1952: The Democrats drafted Adlai Stevenson."

The second of these themes has been used for a long time, too. Indeed, the identification of the candidate with the great men of the nation's past has crystallized into a sort of political litany. With monotonous regularity the sacred names of the political hagiology are invoked in behalf of the candidate. One must take pause before condemning as a politician this candidate who models himself upon Washington, Jefferson, Jackson, or Lincoln; else he may find himself guilty by clear logical implication of the monstrous impiety of disparaging the chief figures in the pantheon of the Republic.

The lengths to which this identification are carried are sometimes ludicrous in the extreme. Bryan's biographers asserted that "Artists have made much over the resemblance of Bryan to Washington. With a wig properly placed, the resemblance is startling." The life of John W. Davis, it seemed, exhibited a unique similarity to that of Jefferson. Beginning with the coincidence of their being born on the same day of the year, his biographer listed an entire page of "similarities," and concluded, rather wistfully, with the admission that Davis never became as "expert" a violinist as Jefferson had been. Observing that an editorial writer had referred to Willkie as "the Abe Lincoln of Wall Street," his biographer modestly concurred: "There is something of Lincoln about him."

The early biographies were by no means free of this effort to depict the candidate as a reincarnation of the great hero. Their concentration, however, is upon the fact that the great hero knew and approved of the candidate. Jefferson was alleged to have endorsed Clay's candidacy thus: " 'As for Mr. Clay, I consider him to be one of the most talented and brilliant men and Statesmen that the country has ever produced, and should I live many years longer, I hope to see him hold the place of chief executive of the American republic.' " In the two decades before the Civil War, Jackson was the hero from whom the candidate secured a political blessing. Recording

112

Lewis Cass's pilgrimage to the Hermitage in 1844, his anonymous biographer concluded: "He may almost be said to have received the last political adieu and teachings of the veteran. . . ." Interestingly, there were no attempts in the biographies of the 1870's and 1880's to suggest that Lincoln blessed the political future of a candidate.

There are, of course, other lesser saints in this political litany whose names are invoked with reverence. Ben Franklin, Madison, Clay, and Cleveland are appealed to several times each. Perhaps it is worth noting that Alexander Hamilton was called upon but once (in a biography of Hoover) and then not especially enthusiastically. But no others can approach the popularity of Washington, Jefferson, Jackson, and Lincoln. Moreover, their intercession is entreated just as fervently today as it was when they were living elder statesmen. If anything, the piety of the invocation deepens as the years lengthen. It is notable, too, that for the most part, they seem to be the exclusive property of no one party. With Washington, and to a large extent with Jefferson, this is easily understood. But it must cause considerable irritation in Republican circles to find Democratic candidates calling upon the name of Lincoln. The biographers of Bryan, Wilson, and Stevenson, especially, have made free with the Great Emancipator. No Republican candidate's campaign biographer has attempted to retaliate by stealing Andrew Jackson—he is, since the Civil War, a thoroughly partisan saint.

With very few exceptions, the pattern has been unvarying: the candidate is a statesman (a politician transfigured) of the ilk of the great heroes of the past; where it is possible that a laying on of hands could take place during the great hero's lifetime, it does indeed take place; where this is manifestly impossible the candidate takes the hero for his model and faithfully reflects his great qualities.

In broad perspective the handling of the political life of candidates from Jackson to the current crop of hopefuls exhibits a remarkable consistency. Almost from the beginning the biographer must defend the candidate—on the personal level against the charge that he is a mere politician, on the institutional level against the charge that he is a mere instrument of a political party. Since it is impossible to deny, in most instances, that he is a politician and a member of a political party, the biographers insist that wholesale condemnation of politicians and parties is not fair. There are good politicians and good party politics. Both are defined in negative terms. A good poli-

113

tician is not a time-server, not a place-seeker, not an intriguer, not a professional. A good party man is not a party tool, not a man who will sacrifice principle to party demands, not a selfish partisan, not a member of a political machine. Two themes used by the biographer in describing the political career of the candidate are positive in nature and permit him to retake the offensive. One is that the office has sought the man and the other is that the candidate is a contemporary version of one of the great political heroes of the nation's past. These two themes enable the biographer to complete the discussion of this episode of the life of the candidate on a note of triumphant vindication.

The evolution in the handling of the candidate's career in public office, noted along the way, has been slight. From 1824 to 1840 the word politician seemed to conjure up no vision of a low, cunning placeman. After 1840 there is little room for doubt that it becomes a term of opprobrium. The "amateur in politics" appears to be becoming not only increasingly popular but increasingly bold. Amateurs since Wilson are playing up their *skill in politics*. Before 1870 machine politics and "bossism" do not put in an appearance. Since that time they have received a good deal of attention. Finally, until 1952 the perennially popular theme that the office sought the man was treated with no hesitant self-consciousness. There is now some indication that this might not meet the unquestioning acceptance of the voter-reader.

That the disapproval of the politician, the distrust of party politics, and the general impression that "politics is a dirty business" found in the campaign biographies reflect deeply rooted ideas in American life, no one would question. These prejudices have been continuously noted by innumerable observers, foreign and domestic, of the American scene. Moreover, the vast significance of the nation's adherence to these ideas—especially at the present, when almost no area of life remains unaffected by government—has been repeatedly dwelt upon. To many this has been a source of inestimable woe and they have pleaded with their fellow citizens to end the conditions that make these prejudices only too well grounded in fact. To other, keener, analysts of the nation's political life, the prejudices appear not entirely without factual basis but grossly exaggerated be-

Character and Public Services

OF

ABRAHAM· LINCOLN.

BY

WILLIAM M. THAYER,

AUTHOR OF THE "PIONEER BOY," THE "YOUTH'S HISTORY OF THE REBELLION," ETC.

BOSTON:

DINSMOOR AND COMPANY,

33, School Street.

1864.

Title page from *Character and Public Services of Abraham Lincoln*

From *Our Standard-Bearer: or, The Life of General Ulysses S. Grant*

"The house is a mere shanty," wrote Oliver Optic, describing the birthplace of Grant, "but it was a good enough house for so great a man to be born in, and compares very favorably with that in which Lincoln, his co-laborer in the war, first drew the breath of life."

From *Life and Speeches of William McKinley*

Major McKinley's mother. "To see her," his biographer wrote, "you must imagine a bright-eyed, motherly old lady, dressed in soft black, with a white lace collar around the throat and a cap of snow-white on her head."

From *The Early Life and Public Career of James A. Garfield*

"Young Garfield conquering a peace." Since the Civil War the
idea of boyhood has changed markedly from the ante-bellum
Lord Fauntleroy pattern.

From *The Early Life and Public Career of James A. Garfield*

"During a minor battle of the Civil War the hero [James A. Garfield] found himself holding the balance; both sides were wavering; 'he turns his eyes to the northward, his lips tighten, he pulls off his coat and throws it into the air and it lodges in a tree top out of reach, then he says to his men: Boys, *we* must go at them.'"

Calvin Coolidge "haying" in Vermont. The biographers are convinced that the appeal of the sturdy yeoman, the simple republican farmer, as a symbol of honesty, integrity, instinctive democracy, and almost mystical capacity for statesmanship is deeply rooted in the fiber of the American mind and constitutes therefore a continuing political asset.

From *William Howard Taft,*
The Man of the Hour

"Mr. Taft as a golf player." As early as 1908 the pattern that persists to the present had been established in the biographies as it has become established in the national mind: give your all to make the team in high school and college; keep fit after college with tennis or, preferably, golf; and root for the home team and the alma mater as a spectator.

From *Life and Public Services of James G. Blaine*

"Blaine at home—under the apple trees." Neither rich nor poor, the candidate leads a quiet, moral, enjoyable, but unostentatious life—standing foursquare for God, Home, and Mother.

cause of a profoundly unrealistic view of the operation of American politics.

It has been pointed out that between 1824 and 1840 the campaign biographers did not regard the fact that the candidate was a politician as a cause for alarm. There is no elaborate defense of this aspect of the candidate's career. Beginning in 1840 there is a dawning awareness that the politician may not be universally esteemed. From this time on there is an increasingly elaborate effort made in campaign lives to convince the voter-reader that although the candidate is a politician, he is not *what one usually thinks of as a politician.*

The task of suggesting an explanation for the origin of the prejudice against the politician can thus be narrowed to a search for the causes of this change during the period 1824 to 1840. And if the biographies are an accurate reflection of the culture to which they were addressed, the area to be searched should be the political life of the nation during these years.

It is commonly accepted that a crucial change in American political life took place in the 1830's. One aspect of this change was the appearance on the American political scene of the professional politician. His appearance and the factors that account for his origin and growth go far toward providing an explanation for the popular revulsion against him. The factors that produced him are in part the same factors that produced the change in the American political scene of the age of Jackson. They are all common coin among political historians.

For a starting point it is not necessary to go beyond the broadening of the franchise that had taken place between 1800 and the 1830's in the constitutions of the newer states and in the revisions of older state constitutions. With the widening of the electorate came a lowering of the tone of campaigning and the beginning of "circus politics." With the achievement of victory by the employment of these political methods to mobilize the newly enfranchised came the introduction of the spoils system, designed to ensure continual victories. Along with the broadening of the franchise in the states, the same wind of democratic enthusiasm brought a vast proliferation of elective offices. This quite naturally complicated the task of voting and expanded the volume of electioneering. A new business was born—a business devoted to the production of candidates to fill public office and to supply the machinery to have them elected. The

115

specialized skills required to tend this machinery and to supervise the production of candidates was beyond the purview of the ordinary citizen. Thus a new occupation, providing full-time employment, was born—professional politics.

Other changes that have a bearing on the explanation of this prejudice were taking place in the economic and social life of the nation. By the 1830's the domain of business enterprise had enlarged its frontiers to include a relatively new and extremely promising field of activity—manufacturing. Particularly in the Northeast beginnings were substantial enough to provide a strong attraction for men of talent. Finally, during the 1830's the old habit of deference to one's betters gave way to a maturing democratic analysis of society based upon the assumption of the equal worth of every man.

Although each of these factors was the result of slow growth, the coincidence of their culmination or intensification in this period gives to the era an appearance of being quite revolutionary. It is not difficult to see how a revulsion for politics and the politician would arise in the more cultivated circles of American society and why "gentlemen" would turn to more seemly pursuits, leaving the field to the professional. Summarizing the results of these changes, Carl Russell Fish concludes: "In the Northeast was the greatest change. Here the revolt against aristocracy was keenest. The public tended to reject the candidate of wealth and social position, while the character of the contests rendered politics unfashionable. . . . This attitude not only kept the supercilious out of politics, but meant that politics was not a road to social recognition for the untutored. It had much less to offer financially or in distinction than the new forms of industrial activity. It attracted on the whole the less favorably placed and the less able."

It is a more difficult matter, however, to explain how the scorn for the politician obtained a wide currency, if indeed it did, among ordinary folk. For certainly it is indisputable that most of the factors mentioned above as productive of the changes on the political scene were in essence democratic reforms designed to enlarge popular participation in government. Nevertheless there is a great irony lurking in the changes wrought in these years that makes the possibility that this scorn was shared by the ordinary folk not entirely ridiculous. As has been noted, the same factors that brought about a democratization of American politics also made inevitable the advent of the

116

professional politician. As early as 1898 one of the foremost political scientists, Henry Jones Ford, commenting on the irony, concluded that "It may be laid down as a political maxim, that whatever assigns to the people a power which they are naturally incapable of wielding takes it away from them."

In contrast to this gradual evolution of scorn for the politician, a distrust and disdain of political parties was a widely shared attitude long before the advent of Jacksonian democracy. In the campaign biographies this hostility to party appears from the very beginning and continues to the present. While there is little discernible evolution in the handling of this theme, it can be noted, as a general impression, that the bitterest denunciations of party appear in the earlier biographies and the most ardent championing of the good points of party appear in the more recent ones.

Hostility toward political parties was a decided part of the heritage of ideas brought by the colonists from an England that had suffered from the abuses of party strife and the machinations of factions for generations. In the eighteenth century all of the ills from which old England suffered were laid at the door of partisanship by the English Whig publicists. This Whig analysis of politics has left a permanent mark on American attitudes toward government.

There was, to be sure, plenty of political activity in the colonies before the Revolutionary crisis but little that could be regarded as true party politics on a continental scale. The Revolution not only produced the first "national" political parties but also served to reinforce the prejudice against party in a thoroughgoing fashion. The party of the opposition were traitors! The successful conclusion of the Revolution left, of course, only the triumphant Whigs.

Historians of party politics believe it is misleading to refer to the friends and foes of the Constitution as contending parties. Indeed, both sides shared the deep prejudice against the existence of party. The old Whig abhorrence of party spirit raged in the bosoms of the fathers. Their speeches and correspondence teem with illustrations of this dread of "faction." The *Federalist* abounds with denunciations of "the pestilential influence of party animosities." The chief architect of the Constitution devoted one entire number of the *Federalist Papers* to the danger of faction. Madison begins his famous "Federalist Number 10" with the statement: "Among the numerous advantages promised by a well-constructed Union, none deserves to

117

be more accurately developed than its tendency to break and control the violence of faction." All his life, John Adams, one of the Constitution's staunchest friends, had reflected on "the rancor of that fiend, the spirit of party . . . [which] wrought an entire metamorphosis of the human character . . . destroyed all sense and understanding, all equity and humanity, all memory and regard to truth, all virtue, honor, decorum, and veracity." The spirit of party was just as roundly denounced by foes of the Constitution like Richard Henry Lee, who warned his fellow citizens that the new instrument of government would not adequately protect them "from the conduct of . . . unprincipled parties . . . between which honest and substantial people have long found themselves situated."

With the beginning of the Republic comes the beginning of American party politics. Again, however, there is a reluctance to consider the Federalist party a national party in the modern sense. It was a "party of leaders" rather than a "party of voters." It lacked any thoroughgoing organization, and it lacked a broad base of appeal. But even more important for the purpose of this discussion, it lacked in its early years an opposition.[1] Its leaders vigorously denied that it was a party; they condemned the idea of party; and when an opposition party did arise, they sincerely held to the old Whig notion that the opposition could have no other purpose but to destroy the state. "Nothing," wrote John Marshall, "I believe more debases or pollutes the human mind than faction." And even after the opposition had been in power for seven years, the high priest of Federalism refused to admit that his fears were groundless: "Our days," wrote Fisher Ames in 1808, "are made heavy with the pressure of anxiety, and our nights restless with visions of horror." Perhaps the classic statement of the Federalist view on "the baneful effects of the spirit of party generally" is contained in Washington's Farewell Address. "This spirit," he warned, "unfortunately, is inseparable from our nature, having its roots in the strongest passions of the human mind. It exists under different shapes in all Governments, more or less stifled, controuled, or repressed; but, in those of the popular form

[1] Two recent studies have provided some challenging evidence on the early beginnings of national political parties that may require their dating to 1800 at the latest. See Joseph Charles, *The Origins of the American Party System: Three Essays* (Williamsburg, 1956) and Noble E. Cunningham, Jr., *The Jeffersonian Republicans: The Formation of Party Organization, 1789–1801* (Chapel Hill, 1958).

118

it is seen in its greatest rankness and is truly their worst enemy. The alternate domination of one faction over another, sharpened by the spirit of revenge natural to party dissension, which in different ages and countries has perpetrated the most horried enormities, is itself a frightful despotism. But this leads at length to a more formal and permanent despotism. The disorders and miseries, which result, gradually incline the minds of men to seek security and repose in the absolute power of an Individual. . . ."

Before 1800, when control of the government passed from one party of leaders to another, one of the greatest tasks of Jefferson's Republican party was to distinguish its opposition to the administration from disloyalty to the government provided by the Constitution. When, in his first inaugural, Jefferson said, "We are all Republicans; we are all Federalists," this was no mere pleasantry. "It is obvious," one political historian sagely observes, "that intended as a statement of the fact of an identity of partizanship it was simply not so; and had it been intended as a kindly sentiment used in persuasion it would have been too fatuous for any conceivable success. Jefferson's use of this simple statement in his first official utterance is excellent evidence of his still persisting thought that he and his party were as yet on the defensive in the United States; that is, on the defensive in existing as a party."

But Jefferson's words could not banish the prejudice. In 1816 Jackson wrote to President-elect Monroe: "Everything depends upon the selecting of your ministry . . . in every selection party and party feeling ought to be laid out of view (for now is the time to put them down). . . ." Later that year a letter of Monroe in reply to Jackson clearly indicates that the idea of a loyal opposition was not yet accepted: "We have heretofore been divided into two great parties. That some of the leaders of the Federal Party entertained principles unfriendly to our system of government I have been thoroughly convinced; and that they meant to work a change in it, by taking advantage of favorable circumstances, I am equally satisfied." After hinting darkly that he has positive proof of this, he concludes: "Many men . . . are of the opinion that . . . free government cannot exist without parties. This is not my opinion." Finally, as late as 1825 John Quincy Adams, in his inaugural, is still holding forth the old Whig ideal: "There still remains one effort of magnanimity, one sacrifice of prejudice and passion, to be made by the individuals

119

throughout the nation who have heretofore followed the standards of political party. It is that of discarding every remnant of rancor against each other, of embracing as countrymen and friends, and of yielding to talents and virtue alone that confidence which in times of contention for principle was bestowed only upon those who bore the badge of party communion."

Thus by the time that national political parties in the modern sense became established in the United States, in the 1830's, there was a tradition of long duration that regarded them as evil. And despite the realization of their necessity for the operation of our form of government and the manifold services they render to the political health of the nation, the prejudice has lived on. The only alteration is the recognition that, although evil, they are a necessary evil.

In faithfully reflecting the prejudices of the nation against politicians and political parties, the campaign biographies are at odds with many serious scholars of American politics who regard the politician and the party as not only essential but decidedly beneficial to the health of the nation's political life. No such division of opinion exists in connection with the ideal that the office should seek the man. Whatever the reality has been and continues to be, this ideal must remain a cardinal belief in the creed of any democrat. Public office is an honor and a duty. As an honor, it cannot be sought after. The dagger of Brutus must be ever alert to ambition or the Republic will perish. As a duty, it cannot be shirked. No one has the right to make the statement attributed to William Tecumseh Sherman: "If nominated I will not run; if elected I will not serve." To attempt any further explanation of this ideal seems unnecessary.

Equally obvious is the campaign biographer's appeal to the memory of the nation's great statesmen. That the candidate's heroes are the nation's heroes admits of no doubt. They have withstood the erosion of time. From the early naive veneration, through the blasts of debunking biographers, to the measured brush strokes of mature scholarship, the brightness of their halos has emerged undimmed in the eyes of the nation. They fill a real need in a nation whose firm dissenting Protestantism and staunch republican convictions cut itself off from the traditional symbolism of Western civilization. To personify the idea of the nation, the principles upon which it was founded and hopes to endure, Americans have selected Washington,

120

Jefferson, Jackson, and Lincoln. The degree of identity that can in truth be made between the man and the symbol has proved completely inconsequential.

The process through which these republican saints have been canonized has been explored learnedly by several scholars. They have observed that despite torrents of abuse during the heroes' public careers, all but Lincoln were well on their way to glory before they died, and Lincoln's ascent began immediately after. The passing years have built about them an accretion of myth. Literature and the plastic arts have embalmed and embroidered the myth. The end product has been a well-developed cult devoted to each of the heroes.

There is little more than an academic interest in pointing to the irony involved in the campaign biographer's attempt to make his candidate something more than a politician by comparing him to Washington, Jefferson, Jackson, or Lincoln, all of whom, except Washington, were masterful politicians. This is but to confuse the man with the symbol. The politician was buried with the man; the statesman lives in symbol.

PART FIVE: Everyman

10————

THE FIRESIDE VIRTUES

A Glimpse of the Candidate at Home

BEFORE TAKING LEAVE OF HIS READERS THE CAMPAIGN BI-
ographer nearly always sketches one final scene that provides a
glimpse of the candidate at home. This is an intimate close-up and
the biographers often drop their grave demeanor and attempt to
become witty and charming.

Although the character of these little excursions into the candidate's very private world seem, on the surface, to partake strongly
of the nature of a miscellany of odds and ends that could not be
worked in elsewhere, they do have a unity of purpose that is of considerable importance. Their aim is to present the candidate as
Everyman. This, obviously, is an abrupt change of pace. After several
hundred pages extolling the achievements that have marked the
candidate as a man at least several cuts above the ordinary, the
reader discovers at the end that he is just a plain, simple man, exactly
like himself. Neither rich nor poor, the candidate leads a quiet,
moral, enjoyable, but unostentatious life—standing foursquare for
God, Home, and Mother. "And right here is the immense value of
the man . . . ," wrote Theodore Roosevelt's biographer, "who will
stand like a rock for the homely virtues, for the Ten Commandments,
in good and evil report, and refuse to budge."

Only rarely will a campaign biographer manifest any qualms about
invading the privacy of the candidate. "A very wholesome theory
that a man's home is his castle and that the sanctuary of private life
is one that must be respected has no application in America to a
public man," wrote the biographer of Bryan. There is, the biographers feel, sound reasoning behind the people's right to know: "The
American people," as one of them put it, "still believe that a man
who does not fulfill his obligations to the community as a good husband and father, and an honorable man of business, cannot be fit to

administer the highest office in the gift of the people. . . . The home life of a man, and those who make his home life, have much to do, it is maintained, with his success." This is a belief not likely to pass out of currency. It is, as "Mr. Hoover thoroughly understands," his biographer revealed, a "simple yet profound truth that the government of a democratic people cannot rise beyond the heights of their home life."

While the candidate would undoubtedly lead the same simple, homey kind of life regardless of his financial circumstances, it is always made emphatically clear that he is not a rich man.[1] On the other hand, because he is a man of uncommon ability he has, naturally, achieved a measure of financial success. Seldom is he described as poor. The candidate's financial condition is usually spoken of as "comfortable" or as a "modest competency." Some biographers go further and estimate the candidate's worldly goods in dollars and cents. Pierce was "not today worth ten thousand dollars"; Garfield was worth $15,000 to $18,000; Cleveland, $50,000; and Bryan, $110,000 to $125,000. A favorite theme is the candidate grown "poor" in the service of his country. In 1836 it was written of William Henry Harrison: "He not only exposed his life, and gave his labour to his country, but contributed a portion of his estate to sustain her in one of the darkest periods of her existence. . . ." In 1928 a biographer could take pride in reporting Hoover's remark, "I think I'm broke," after his years of uncompensated service during World War I.

In keeping with his modest competency the candidate owns a simple but comfortable home. "At home, he [Lincoln] lives like a gentleman of modest means and simple tastes. A good-sized house of wood, simply but tastefully furnished, surrounded by trees and flowers, is his own, and there he lives, at peace with himself, the idol of his family, and for his honesty, ability, and patriotism, the admiration of his countrymen." Descriptions, sometimes minute, of the candidates' homes occur frequently in the biographies. The house itself is always unpretentious, free from any signs of ostentatious display. Typically, as in the case of the Hayes home, "there is not a

---

[1] The exception was James M. Cox: "Governor Cox is the only man ever nominated for President," confessed one of his biographers, "who owns wealth—real wealth." The nearest approach to this admission occurs in a biography of Alton B. Parker, whose financial condition was described as "very moderately rich."

tower, nor balcony, nor finial, nor filagree of any kind." Inside, the furnishings are "tasteful," never ornate; in general, like the Garfield home, "everything about the place, while plain and unpretentious, gives it an appearance of quiet comfort." During the second half of the nineteenth century, the biographer frequently conducted the reader from room to room, describing the contents of each. By the nineteen twenties this had been abandoned. In its stead has come a far more effective device that not only achieves the earlier biographers' aim to show the candidate's Spartan simplicity, but also manages to link him with objects that have high associational value. A biographer of Coolidge has achieved a masterpiece: "Here are some of the properties which he [a hypothetical caller] found in the background of the family life: book-strewn table; rug of standard pattern; framed photographic copy of Sir-Galahad; photograph of Crawford Notch; Bible history; sewing-bag; a lidless graphophone, with no operatic records; bric-a-brac; bay window with blinds tied back; ice-card; parchesi; hooks with boys' hats, baseballs, bats and gloves; dog; gas stove; fireplace with wood ashes, and over it this sentiment—

A wise old owl lived in an oak:
The more he saw the less he spoke.
The less he spoke the more he heard:
Why can't we be like that old bird?"

The center of all this domesticity is the candidate's wife. Increasingly she has been developed as a candidate for First Lady. While still primarily a homemaker and companion to her husband, considerably more attention is being paid to her as a potential mistress of the White House with all of the social obligations and public appearances this entails.

Until the 1870's the candidate's wife received little more than passing attention. In a sentence or two, the reader was assured that she was an excellent woman who had been faithfully devoted to her husband through many years of toil and of happiness. An 1836 biographer of William Henry Harrison provides a typical comment for this early period: Mrs. Harrison "has been the faithful companion of this distinguished patriot during the various perils and vicissitudes of his eventful life, and lives to witness the maturity of his fame, and the honors paid him by a grateful country."

Beginning with Lucy Hayes the amount of detail devoted to the candidate's wife grows appreciably. It is interesting to note that as her fitness for the "public office" of First Lady comes increasingly to be emphasized, there is also an intensification of the insistence on her domesticity. Mrs. Hayes exhibited many talents, social graces, and enlightened views on current topics but she was also "the true housewife, the noble consort, the faithful Christian mother." The idea that the biographers attempt to convey is that although equal to the social obligations that will be her lot to bear, she is no frivolous social butterfly. Take the case of Lucretia Garfield: "Much of the time that other women give to distributing visiting cards, in the frantic effort to make themselves 'leaders of society,' Mrs. Garfield spends in the alcoves of the Congressional Library, searching out books to carry home to study while she nurses the children. . . . She has moved . . . in a life of absolute devotion to her duty; never forgetting the demands of her position or neglecting her friends, yet making it her first charge to bless her home, to teach her children . . . to be the equal friend, as well as the honored wife, of her husband."

This sort of thing has continued to the present. Despite her wide range of interests, Eleanor Roosevelt, the reader was assured, did not differ from this general pattern: "A Dutch-housewife wholesomeness pervaded the home. It was well-managed, efficiently planned, pleasantly domestic and warmly cozy." These protestations were apparently unacceptable to FDR's opponents, for in 1944 Eleanor afforded the Dewey biographer an excellent "strawman" to demolish in describing the wife of the Republican candidate: "The truth about Mrs. Dewey," he wrote, "is extraordinarily simple: Without being 'plain,' she shuns display. She has a mind of her own, but she ventures no political opinions except to her closest friends. She makes no speeches. She could make a speech but she sees no reason for making one. She joins none of those organizations, however worthy in purpose, which are dedicated either to the uplift or the annoyance of mankind. She has turned down all offers to write magazine articles, though she could doubtless have put the money to good use. She doesn't even have a secretary. She appears, in short, to have a great deal of common sense."

Part of the process of humanizing the candidate is a gay little sally into the courtship in which he won this paragon of wifely virtue. Apparently the possibilities of the ancient saw, "all the world loves a lover," were neglected for a very long time, for not until near the end of the nineteenth century is the reader permitted to go a-wooing with the candidate.

It seems particularly inappropriate that this emphasis on romance should begin with Cleveland. Yet the middle-aged, corpulent statesman, the confessed sire of a bastard child, titillated the nation with his courtship of a young college girl that ended in a White House wedding. In his campaign for re-election, Cleveland's biographers had a field day describing the wedding in minute detail. Given Cleveland's past, it seems a lack of delicacy to have included the following bit of minutiae: ". . . a scroll, composed of pinks and bearing the national motto, 'E Pluribus Unum,' was fixed immediately above the center doorway."

From Cleveland's time onward the candidate must tread the boards for at least one brief scene in which he is cast as a lover. Even the austere Wilson had his moment. Speaking of the courtship that culminated in his first marriage, one of his biographers easily leads the field in cloying cuteness: "It is about this time that this most natural sort of man did another most natural thing. The balmy Southern air is conducive, so the poets say, to dreams filled with emotion, tenderness, and romance. They tell us that in the Sunny South the azure skies azure a little bit more than they do in any other part of the country. . . . He had made an occasional trip to Savannah, Georgia, where dwelt a charming Southern lady of rare beauty and accomplishments; and, a short time before Woodrow Wilson became Ph.D., he also received another degree, and became Woodrow Wilson, M.M., for he married Miss Ellen Louise Axson, of a distinguished Savannah family, descended from the Cavaliers." Aware that the spectacle of Cal Coolidge masquerading as Romeo would be too ludicrous to down, his biographer remarked dourly on his marriage to a teacher at the Clark School for the Deaf in Northampton: "The humorous gifts of many have also been taxed to set off the appropriateness of Mrs. Coolidge's transition from the old charge to the new."

To return to the fireside circle, the scene is, of course, incomplete without children. Children and dogs love the candidate. The emphasis is naturally upon the candidate's own children and grandchildren but not to the exclusion of children generally. One biographer wrote of Lincoln: "He was always on the best of terms with children, as the little folks of Springfield, where he lived so long, will testify. He loved them, and they loved him. . . ." The reader was assured that Benjamin Harrison's "fondness for children is not limited to his own descendant. Every boy and girl in the neighborhood knows him and loves him, as he knows and loves them all. . . . There is something in his kindly way and protecting manner that must have a peculiar charm for childhood." But the palm goes to a biographer of Theodore Roosevelt for this anecdote demonstrating the candidate's love of children: "Then I see him as he stood that day on the car platform at Greenport, shaking hands with the school children that came swarming down just as the train was going to pull out. I see him spy the forlorn little girl in the threadbare coat, last among them all, who had given up in dumb despair, for how could she ever reach her hero through that struggling crowd, with the engineer even then tooting the signal to start? And I see him leap from the platform and dive into the surging tide like a strong swimmer striking from the shore, make a way through the shouting mob of youngsters clear to where she was on the outskirts looking on hopelessly, seize and shake her hand as if his heart were in his, and then catch the moving train on a run, while she looked after it, her pale, tear-stained face one big happy smile. That was Roosevelt every inch of him, and don't you like him too?"

Generally the reader is not carried to such heights of melodrama. Indeed, before 1860 there was virtually no mention of children—the candidate's or anyone else's. Since 1860 the candidate is usually pictured as spending a part of each busy day romping with his children or grandchildren. He does not "spoil" them, of course. They often attend the public schools just like the children of other plain folks. And like other children they do odd jobs to earn spending money.

This glimpse of the candidate's private world invariably includes a mention of his religion and often a discussion of his morals. From 1824 to 1960 there is a remarkable consistency on the subject of the candidate's religion. He is deeply reverent but never sanctimonious. Although he is an "orthodox Christian," he is not narrowly sectarian. Above all he is tolerant—a firm believer in religious freedom.

There is a vagueness about the handling of the candidates' religious faith that makes further analysis of it difficult. Yet the impression emerges that this vagueness does not emanate from any design to deceive. It is, rather, that sincere vagueness that appears to be endemic to religion in America—a nation that has spawned the most sects and the fewest theologians.

Looking more closely at these generalizations, at least one or two observations can be made to give them a more concrete meaning. There is, to begin with, a firm belief in God. And moreover, it is a distinctly Christian conception of God, for the biographers leave little doubt that the candidate holds to the idea of a Divine Providence that takes a hand in the affairs of men. Still further, His interposition may be enlisted by prayer, and for whatever good befalls one, He should be thanked. Thus, no biographer of Jackson failed to point up the day of thanksgiving ordered by the hero after the victory at New Orleans. "Respited from the arduous duties of the field, his first concern was to draw the minds of all in thankfulness and adoration to that sovereign mercy, without whose aid, and inspiring counsel, vain would be all earthly efforts." Lincoln, his 1864 biographers emphasized, "has embraced every opportunity to publicly acknowledge the source from whence have come all the blessings the people of the Union have received during the progress of the Civil war. . . ."

This is not free thought, agnosticism, or Deism—this is orthodoxy. But it is also nonsectarian. In essence the principle that can be extracted from countless expressions on the subject in the campaign biographies boils down to this: religion is only a personal matter between each man and God in so far as it involves a choice of a Christian sect; but while it is important that such a choice be made, it does not matter which sect is chosen. There is no exclusive path to salvation. McKinley, for example, "may be seen every Sunday at the Methodist church. He believes in Christianity, but he has never made capital of his religion, and there is nothing of the Pharisee about him. On the other hand, he has a deep religious side to his nature. He has nothing to do with the infidelity and free thought which are so common among many of our public men, and he never says anything against religion, even in jest." Thus, it is a rare campaign biography that does not insist that the candidate is a regular Sunday church goer. Often he teaches a Sunday-school class. But it is not essential that he be a communicant or a member; he might even be a regular attendant of a church of a different denomination from his own.

This spirit goes beyond toleration. Toleration is reserved for Roman Catholics. From the 1850's onward, whenever biographers wax eloquent on the fierce passion for religious toleration that burns in the bosom of their heroes, the examples of its practical application always involve Roman Catholics. Pierce fought the good fight for repeal of the religious test in the New Hampshire constitution. Stephen A. Douglas thundered against the Know-Nothings. "It was the first speech ever delivered in the United States by any prominent public man, since the organization of the Know-Nothing party, against the proscriptive principles of that party." Dewey would get up early on Sunday mornings to drive the daughter of a country neighbor to Mass when her parents were away. While none of the biographies contain anything that could be construed as anti-Semitism, only one, a biography of Theodore Roosevelt, makes a specific point of extending religious toleration to Judaism.

Examination of the morals of the candidate is ordinarily not part of the discussion of religion in the campaign biographies but is a distinct topic in itself. The Christian wellspring of ethical conduct is either taken for granted or else morality is assumed to require no more than a secular basis. If the latter is true, it would be a very difficult thing to document. There occurs only one clear expression: "Mr. Van Buren," his biographer stated, "has ever been an exemplary and strict observer of those moral rules which are essential to the well-being and decorum of society." On the other hand, the candidate's honesty, generosity, and integrity are not usually pointed up as proof of his Christianity, but rather as indication of his civic worth and private character. Quite apart from any reward to which this conduct might entitle him in the hereafter, it is clear that he expects to be rewarded by his fellow citizens here and now.

Honesty, generosity, and integrity are virtues that have been universally prized in Western civilization and it is hardly surprising to find that Americans hope they will be found in the men they select for public office. But campaign biographers do not rest the matter of morality here. From 1836 to the present they have persistently presented the candidate as a man of rectitude in matters that seem to be of peculiarly American concern. These "vices" of which the

132

candidate is singularly free are intemperance, profanity, gambling, and, to some extent, smoking. When William Henry Harrison entered the army "the practice of drinking spirits was universal; public sentiment had not denounced it as immoral, nor was intoxication considered, as it is now, degrading to the character of the gentleman." But despite these temptations to drink and also to gamble, "Mr. Harrison had the good sense to see and avoid these dangers." Winfield Scott "was among the very earliest pioneers in the effort to do something to check and prevent the enormous evil of intemperance." He published an essay on intemperance in the *National Gazette* (December 22, 1821) and his arguments were "adopted by many of the original temperance advocates and temperance societies." Of Lincoln his biographer wrote: "'He has no vices,' remarked a distinguished statesman; and the remark is true. His most intimate friend never witnessed the least approximation to a vice in Mr. Lincoln. He never smokes, never uses intoxicating drinks, never utters a profane word, or engages in games of chance." In 1868 the voter-reader was asked to believe that Grant "drank nothing stronger than cold water. . . ." His excessive smoking was excused by another of his biographers as "a necessity . . . of his physical system. . . ."

This exoneration of the candidate from the vices of intemperance, smoking, gambling, and profanity continues down to Coolidge. Here, again, as in the case of his piety, the candidate makes no parade of his purity of habits. Typical of this understanding forbearance of sinners was Bryan, "a man who does not smoke, yet who does not hesitate, on occasion, to offer cigars to his friends; who will sit hour after hour in tobacco-laden air, sharing in the conversation of those whose mouths are chimneys for the time. He never drinks wine or liquor, yet he never flaunted a phylactery, or called names when the clink of glasses was heard. In all things a temperate and abstemious man, yet, such is his toleration that there is nothing oppressive about his being better than most of us."

This tolerance has served to save the candidate from saintliness or prudery—traits of character not apt to find favor in the eyes of his fellow citizens. Consider the plight of one biographer who had built Theodore Roosevelt into such a shining knight that he himself was aghast. "And has he no faults, this hero of mine?" he exclaimed. "Yes," he answered, "he has and I am glad of it, for I want a live

133

man for a friend, not a dead saint. . . ." The faults of Theodore, it developed were: "he cannot dance" and "I have heard him sing—that he cannot do."

Recently a new trend in "morality" is being established. It no longer relies on tolerance of other people's vices or scraping the bottom for faults like Theodore's to establish the fact that the hero is flesh and blood. The candidate now merely indulges in "the vices" to a moderate degree. Dewey has "been known to swear. As a cusser, however, he is adjudged by experts to be less than adept. . . . he seldom plays poker, and then only for small stakes; he is never spectacularly successful. He will take a drink or two, preferably Scotch and water, but he has always gone easy on the alcohol."

The absence of these vices, or the recent moderation of his indulgence in them, is in keeping with the essential simplicity of the candidate. This note of republican simplicity is usually the signal for the final curtain. For a brief instant before the curtain descends, he stands alone upon the stage, a splendid figure, the true American, and, in the nineteenth century, a noble product of the wilderness uncorrupted by the decadence of Europe. His uncomplicated nature, genuineness, and natural gentility stand revealed in his unpretentious manner and his plain dress. The words may change but the spirit of this curtain line is always the same. In 1824 it was written of John Quincy Adams: "I shall certainly not contend that he is either a *Petit Maitre* or a *Dandy*; or that he belongs to the still more modern race of the *Corinthian* or the *Exquisite*. He does not trim his mouth to the perpetual smile, nor discipline his head to the ready bow of the sycophant. He does not bely his candour, by expressing an unfelt delight at the intrusion of every impertinent or curious visitor; but still less does he assume the haughty, supercilious, condescending air of vain superiority. . . . Sincerity speaks in every action, too plainly to be misinterpreted: and that should be regarded, among *plain republicans* at least, as a virtue of more worth, than the courtsey which teaches the tongue to utter what the heart denies." In 1952 the statement was couched in a plainer style: "Dwight David Eisenhower is, in all important respects, a simple man"—a man "whose every action reflects the ordinary behavior of his average countryman. . . ."

Throughout the nineteenth century European manners, fashions, and the pomp of royal courts outraged the candidate's simple republicanism. Jackson turned down an appointment as minister to Mexico because he had no stomach for the trappings of the court of Maximilian. When William Henry Harrison was appointed minister to Colombia in 1828, "He was received with the most flattering demonstrations of respect; but his liberal opinions, his stern republican integrity, and the plain simplicity of his dress and manners, contrasted too strongly with the arbitrary opinion and ostentatious behavior of the public officers, to allow him to be long a favorite with those who had usurped the power of that government. They feared that the people would perceive the difference between a real and pretended patriot, and commenced a series of persecutions against our minister, which rendered his situation extremely irksome." Clay, Buchanan, and Douglas were presented as latter-day Benjamin Franklins making their homespun way about the tawdry glitter of European courts. At the end of the century it was a matter of pride to Bryan's campaign biographers that "An English fashion journal objected to the cut of his frock coat on the occasion of a certain public appearance in London. . . ."

In 1824 a campaign biographer had to contend with the charge then current that John Quincy Adams had spent too much time abroad and was, therefore, becoming Europeanized. Over a hundred years later Hoover's biographer was laying about him vigorously to demolish the same charge. "He remained," the biographer insisted, "Yankee of the Yankees—as American as baseball or apple-pie. . . ."

And so they have been simple republicans all. Plain men, scorning fashion, forthright in speech, unpretentious in manner. As American as apple pie, outwardly they are indistinguishable from the man next door. They live comfortably on their modest means, loving their simple homes, enjoying the good fortune of a wife who is equally at home behind the kitchen stove or in the public eye, delighting in their children and those of their neighbors, worshipping God with deep but unostentatious piety, and behaving in a manner that is approved by the moral sense of their community.

To attempt to relate these elements that make up the role of Everyman to cultural ideas and developments over the years would be sheer folly. Most of them are too diffuse, too universally a part of human nature to admit of a search for their origins and a chronicle of their development. Where it has been noted that the use of a particular appeal was not present in the biographies from the beginning, it would be absurd to conclude that the ideas or ideals upon which the appeal is based did not yet exist in American society. Surely Americans rejoiced in a good and capable wife before 1876, believed in romantic love before 1888, and loved children before 1860. Part of the explanation of why those ideas were not exploited previous to these dates may be found in Chapters III and IV, which discuss the evolving prominence of women and children in American society. Perhaps another part of the explanation lies in the increasing interest Americans have come to take in the personal lives of those who aspire to the highest office in the land. This is a trend that stands out with great clarity in an overall view of the campaign biographies, and it will be treated at greater length in the concluding chapter.

CONCLUSION

The Ideal Citizen of the Republic

SURVEYING THE SPRING CROP OF NEW BOOKS FOR *Harper's* in 1952, Charles Poore puzzled over the sickly condition of a once-hardy quadrennial. "What," he inquired, "has happened to the campaign biography? It used to be one of the gaudiest growths of a Presidential year's springtime. . . . Today the form is barely kept alive as candidates stalk office with richly sonorous whither-are-we-drifting collections of speeches and other threnodies of desire."

In 1952 it was certainly difficult to take issue with Mr. Poore's observation. Four years later his words could be recalled as a prophetic utterance. It was almost impossible to find a campaign biography. The doom that he foresaw had become very nearly a reality. Mr. Poore had ventured an explanation for what he called the "vanishing campaign biography." "When Governor Dewey put his suspenders on television, when Senator Kefauver followed with a live crime quiz show, what could books do to keep up with the parade?"

Now, the unexpected has happened: the spring announcements for 1960 reveal a very luxuriant crop. Publishers have promised biographies of Messrs. Richard Nixon, Nelson Rockefeller, Barry Goldwater, John F. Kennedy, Stuart Symington, and Hubert Humphrey.

However, it is still too early to determine whether the campaign biography is making a genuine comeback or not. Certainly the six or seven scheduled for spring publication are a pathetically small representation of a once flourishing form—indeed, preconvention biographies were not included in this examination of campaign biographies, in part because until very recently the vast number of them made the undertaking next to impossible.

Regardless of the ultimate fate of the campaign biography, there

137

is little doubt that its character has changed in recent years. Indeed, it has become a rather difficult task to identify the genuine article. Over the years there have always been a number of authors and publishers who have insisted that their works were not campaign biographies. In most instances this was patently untrue. This is no longer the case. Elements of subtlety were creeping in before 1952, but in that year Noel Busch's *Adlai Stevenson* became something of a milestone with its irreverent handling of a number of the time-honored appeals. By 1960 the gulf of sophistication between the two preconvention biographies that had appeared before this book went to press and the campaign biographies of James A. Garfield is enormous.

Earl Mazo's *Richard Nixon* would certainly not have been "adopted" as a campaign document by the Republican party in 1880 (nor will it likely be in 1960—incidentally, the publisher insists that it is not a campaign biography). Compared to the naive creations of Lew Wallace and Nathaniel Hawthorne, Mr. Mazo's book is a masterpiece of subtlety. There are even passages and incidents related in the book that might be considered anti-Nixon. Speaking of Nixon's campaign tactics, Mr. Mazo says, "Nixon is a practicing Quaker, at home with precepts of kindness to one's fellow man; yet, in fighting for votes, he has resorted to malignant innuendo such as the statement (made during the 1952 campaign) that 'the only way to save America is to get rid of Trumanism, or Stevensonianism, or whatever *ism* with which you choose to tag the whole sorry mess.'" Elsewhere Mazo labels him ambitious for public office, records the facts that his home town refused to name a street in his honor, his college had to form two receiving lines because of those who did not wish to shake his hand after his commencement address, and the faculty of the university at which he had received his law degree vetoed a movement to grant him an honorary degree. These incidents are all related without any attempt to impugn the integrity of the anti-Nixon people involved. Nevertheless, when the reader finishes the book, he has not only a distinctly favorable impression of Nixon as a person but also as presidential timber.

William Manchester's *The Rockefeller Family* represents an entirely different approach, and is even more difficult to label a campaign document. Although it is concerned with three generations of Rockefellers, it concentrates rather heavily on John D., Junior, and Nelson. But the focus is on Nelson. He is the end product in Mr. Manchester's progression: from John D., who made the family fortune, to Junior, who used the fortune to redeem the family name, to Nelson, who combines the energy and leadership ability of his grandfather with the humanitarianism of his father in the interest of the public service. Only one of these three heroes would be out of place among the paragons of the nineteenth-century campaign biography—John D. Even in the case of John D., Mr. Manchester pleads mitigating circumstances while admitting that his client was ultimately responsible for most of the social sins that have been laid to the door of 26 Broadway. Finally, as in the case of Mazo's *Nixon*, the principal hero, Nelson Rockefeller, emerges from these pages as an ideal presidential candidate—not merely one of five brothers of the third generation of Rockefellers. (Mr. Manchester's volume appeared, of course, considerably before Rockefeller's withdrawal from the race for the nomination.)

Admittedly, the "new look" in biographies of political figures who aspire to the presidency is too recent a phenomenon to permit any broad generalizations. It does seem, however, from the short-range point of view, that the campaign biography is not dead but merely undergoing a change in outward form. If the two most recent biographies are examined closely, a considerable number of the appeals dealt with in the foregoing chapters can be discovered. Nixon's ancestry dates from 1690 colonists. "One forefather crossed the Delaware with General Washington and survived a dozen battles of the Revolution." The Rockefellers ignore the Rockefeller Family Association. "They just aren't interested." Nixon was a college footballer and class president; Nelson, "a hustling soccer player" and class vice-president. "In the storied format of poor but honest folks, Nixon's parents gave their five boys each a name, a religion, a political identification, and the basis for a way of life." To a remarkable degree Mr. Manchester's version of the early life of Nelson conforms to this pattern—due, he indicates, to the stern Baptist theology and Poor Richard philosophy of his grandfather. The pattern could be continued through the adult careers of wartime service, through the legal career of Nixon (another lawyer who discouraged litigation) and Nelson (another amateur in politics who is a better politician than the professionals).

All in all, like their predecessors in 136 years of campaign biographies, they turn out to be a symbol—in Sidney Hyman's phrase "the symbol of what Americans as a whole think or wish themselves to be." Certainly they are a far more sophisticated version of the symbol than that stark and primitive image hewn from the life of a Garfield or a Ben Harrison, but, after all, they are addressed to a far more sophisticated reading public.

Nixon and Rockefeller (the latter's public withdrawal from the race notwithstanding) were rivals for the Republican nomination. Yet their respective biographers have presented not two rival symbols but one. And, it is safe to assume, this would be equally true if one of the two was a Democrat and the contest was for the presidency. For if any one implication to be drawn from this analysis is painfully clear, it is that most often rival candidates appear in campaign biographies to be as alike as Tweedledum and Tweedledee. This has always been so. National Republican, Democrat, Whig, and Republican candidates are all presented in much the same way. None of the appeals used by the biographers can be differentiated according to party.

This stubborn fact absolutely ruins the value of this book as a "tout sheet" for picking a winner in an impending presidential election or as a "Monday morning quarterback" lecture for explaining the mistakes of the loser after the contest.

Furthermore, the discovery that party labels are of no importance in determining the way in which presidential candidates are presented in campaign biographies might add strength to the contention of students of American politics who believe that there has always been a decided tendency to exaggerate the differences between the two major parties—a distortion, they believe, of the true situation wherein the area of agreement between the parties dwarfs the area of difference. But it by no means proves this thesis. It must be borne in mind that this conclusion is derived entirely from an analysis of campaign biographies. There are many, many other agencies of persuasion employed in presidential campaigns. It may be that an analysis of any or all of the others might lead to an entirely different set of conclusions regarding the presentation of presidential candidates. Nor has it been demonstrated that the American people have *in fact* been presented with a choice between Tweedledum and Tweedledee every four years from 1824 to 1956. This might be true, but the nature of the evidence examined here certainly does not permit such a conclusion. All that can be asserted is that this is the way they are presented in campaign biographies. Campaign biographies are propaganda. They are not designed as votive offerings to scholarship, intended to serve truth and increase the knowledge of mankind. They are written to serve a definite and immediate purpose—to aid in getting the candidate elected.

It is precisely at this juncture that whatever value this analysis of campaign biographies may have must become apparent. Precisely because these biographies are propaganda directed toward this definite end they are valuable historical material for the student of ideas in America.

That this is their nature and purpose and not a mere assumption deduced from the fact that their publication happens to coincide with the year in which their subjects sought election to the presidency is almost self-evident. No one can read more than a dozen campaign lives without becoming aware of two essential qualities that distinguish them as propaganda rather than biography. The first quality that becomes apparent is that the picture unfolding before the reader is an idealized one, rich in associational value and general appeal but sadly lacking in the penetrating detail, the revealing brush stroke that illumines the uniqueness of the human personality. This alone would prove nothing. But when for the second, third, twelfth, and one hundreth time, the reader encounters the same idealization, the same emphasis on the same things, the conclusion is obvious: these writers are only using a real life as the skeleton upon which to construct an ideal life.

Regarding, then, the scores of campaign biographies examined in the course of this inquiry, it is apparent that they form an unbroken series of attempts, from 1824 to 1960, to fashion an image of the ideal citizen of the Republic. In the construction of this image the biographers have selected and emphasized the things out of the real lives of the candidates that they felt sure would appeal to the voter-reader. For 136 years they have produced a symbol —"a kind of cultural apotheosis in which the nation can see an image of its best aims." Because they have consistently selected and emphasized, with minor variation, the same aspects of the candidates' careers, they provide the student of ideas not only with an image of the ideal whole man but also with a series of ideals involving ancestry, parents, youth, the military, farming, law and business, politics, and the virtues of private home life. The consistent fabrication and employment of these appealing images over this long period of time is the really essential point. It is of little moment for purposes of this inquiry whether all that the biographers wrote was true or false. In either case they remain valuable material for the understanding of American ideas and ideals.

The extent of the liberties that biographers have taken with the facts and the degree of conscious deliberation that accompanied these liberties may justly be regarded as questions irrelevant to this investigation, but not so the question of whether the appeals made by the biographers were in fact to ideas actually held by the American people. No single question is more crucial to the value of this inquiry than the determination of whether the ideas and ideals the candidate is made to represent are ideas and ideals peculiar to his biographer or whether they are shared by the biographer's countrymen. The degree to which the second alternative can be established without qualification is the measure of the value of this investigation to the study of ideas in America.

To prove conclusively that the biographers understood the thought of their contemporaries and directed their appeals to ideas that were widely accepted in American society is a large order. What people have thought is never susceptible to the same sort of proof as what they have said or what they have done. Here, however, is a summary of the circumstantial evidence. The campaign biography has had the intensely practical purpose of helping to win a game in which the stakes were very high. In this game nothing that could be directed was left to chance. The essence of the game was to make the widest possible appeal. There was, then, every incentive to discover and employ that which would appeal. Further, the writers of these biographies were almost invariably men whose ordinary business it was to know what appeals to their countrymen—politicians, journalists, popular writers, and other publicists. They were, in addition, nearly always assisted in their efforts by practical politicians, often including the candidate himself, and the party has frequently subsidized the publication of the biography as an instrument of party propaganda. Finally, there is a considerable amount of direct evidence. As the various ideas and ideals appealed to by the biographers have been sorted out and their development traced, it has been possible to demonstrate in the previous chapters that corresponding ideas and ideals *did in fact* exist in the society toward which these appeals were directed.

In the overall view, the ideal citizen of the Republic who emerges from these thousands of pages is at once a changing and a static figure. Many of the traits that have made up the complete hero have changed over the years. The ideals, of which these traits were but a concretization, have lost their appeal or have been modified in varying degrees. On the other hand, many other characteristics of the ideal citizen have persisted through the years unchanged or only slightly modified. These characteristics appeal to ideals in which the faith of the people appears to be unshaken.

That the figure of the ideal citizen should not remain an entirely constant one over a period of 136 years is hardly startling. If the traditional belief that American society has been an exceedingly dynamic one is correct, this conclusion was certainly to be anticipated. Indeed, in looking back over the changes that have occurred, it is surprising to find that there have been so few that could be regarded as basic or radical changes.

It is difficult to draw any conclusions from an overall view of these changing characteristics. They appear to develop from changes in the idea content of American society. They do not seem to have any relationship one with the other. This is true even of changes that occur simultaneously. For example, 1860 has been remarked as the year from which one can date the beginning of trends toward (1) an increasing emphasis on the mother of the candidate, (2) making the candidate an athlete, and (3) exploiting the candidate's love of children. Thus it is impossible to divide the changing characteristics as a whole into periods or phases of change, labeling changes during one quarter-century as the era of this and the next quarter the era of that. It is even very nearly impossible to detect any direction toward which the whole of the changing characteristics appear to be tending. To conclude that candidates have become increasingly more "liberal" or more "conservative" or more or less "democratic" would not be justified by the evidence. The only observation that can be made is that the sum of these changes has produced an increasingly personal treatment of the candidate. Since the Civil War the tendency is toward an ever expanding amount of detail about the private life of the candidate. Biographers are now peering into every nook and cranny of the candidate's past and present existence as a human being. In 1952 the biographers of both major candidates did not even neglect what their subjects had to eat. In 1960 the voter learned that Nixon "is probably the fastest dresser in high office, with a record of eight minutes for formal clothes and two and a half for regular wear." It might be suggested as an indication that this trend is once more directly attuned to the public mind, that the recent illness of President Eisenhower was treated even more intimately by the daily press. Day after day the public was informed with clinical thoroughness of the physiological details of his life in a hospital bed.

Seen in broad perspective the static characteristics of the ideal citizen are quite another matter. One cannot fail to be struck by the essential similarity in so many respects of all of the candidates as they appeared in campaign biographies between 1824 and 1960. That some characteristics of this symbol should be so fundamental that they would endure down through the years could of course be expected. But that so many, and not a few so little obvious, should endure was decidedly not anticipated. Indeed, so well do these unchanging characteristics cover all the stages of life that it is possible to put a number of them together to produce a summary sketch of the perennial, the enduring candidate. Here in brief is *the* ideal citizen from 1824 to 1960—a presidential candidate that seemingly would have as much appeal to the voter of Jackson's day as to the voter of today: he is a man whose northern European ancestors fought tyranny in the Old World, settled in America before 1776, and gallantly served the patriot cause in the Revolution. His parents are admirable folk, mindful of their duty to rear their son in patriotic virtue and Christian piety. He grows up in humble circumstances, enjoying a happy, active boyhood but one that is not without its struggle to rise, through education and hard work, above the station in life into which he had been born. Midway in this climb to success, he is summoned from his peaceful pursuits to defend his country. Like generations of minutemen before him, he responds instantly and covers himself with glory. His country's hour of peril successfully weathered, he resumes his civilian career. By the time he is nominated, the various occupations he has followed in his struggle to the top have included farming, practicing law, and directing a business enterprise. He has also taken part in the public life of the nation—not, however, as an occupation, but as a service to his community which, as is its right, demanded his talents. As he sits before the hearth in his own unpretentious home awaiting the verdict of the people, one sees a plain, simple man of modest means, surrounded by a dutiful, loving wife and adoring children; a man of practical good sense and boundless energy, a man of deep but unostentatious piety, of impeccable moral character, and of sturdy republican virtue. Certainly, the passage of time has wrought changes in him, and some of these have been significant. But basically he has remained the same—an enduring symbol of the ideals and aspirations of the Republic.

A SELECTED LIST OF
CAMPAIGN BIOGRAPHIES

The following list of campaign biographies makes no pretense of completeness. The circumstances surrounding their publication, described in Chapter I, render it unlikely that a complete list could be assembled. Illustrative of the difficulties that must be surmounted in compiling such a list for only one candidate in one campaign is Ernest J. Wessen's excellent bibliographical study "Campaign Lives of Abraham Lincoln," *Papers in Illinois History . . . 1937* (Springfield, 1938). Wessen has found seventy-eight campaign lives, written in four languages, for the campaign of 1860. The only similar bibliographical study that has been made is Dorothy V. Martin, "William Henry Harrison and the Campaign of 1840: A Check List of Books and Pamphlets," *Annual Report of the Historical and Philosophical Society of Ohio* (Columbus, 1940), 7–21.

The list given below represents all of the campaign biographies from which material has been quoted, plus a representative sampling of the large number of others which also served as the basis for generalizations made in the text. As previously noted, the number of campaign biographies offered to the public has grown increasingly smaller. In 1956 it was difficult to find more than one or two full-length biographies of each of the major party candidates.

The decision to eliminate footnote references to the campaign biographies was made on the basis of the underlying assumption of the book—that it is the sum of these biographies that lends credence to this analysis and the generalizations and conclusions here propounded. Surely, it would be interesting to know, for example, exactly where, in what particular campaign biography of Lincoln, a particular quoted statement is made. But it is not essential. It is of the essence of this study that an almost exact replica of the quotation could have been substituted from any of a number of campaign biographies, ranging in time from 1824 to 1960.

A thoroughly documented copy of this work is available which gives not only the source of the quotations but also a generous sample of the "exact replicas" that could be substituted. This copy is deposited in the library of the University of North Carolina, Chapel Hill, N.C.

1824

Sketch of the Life of John Quincy Adams; taken from the Portfolio of April, 1819; to which are added the Letters of Tell: Originally Addressed to the Editor of the Baltimore American. N.P.: 1824.

EATON, JOHN HENRY. *The Life of Andrew Jackson, Major-General in the Service of the United States; Comprising a History of the War in the South, from the Commencement of the Creek Campaign, to the Termination of Hostilities before New Orleans.* Philadelphia: Samuel F. Bradford, 1824.

1828

Biographical Sketch of the Life of Andrew Jackson, Major-General of the Armies of the United States, the Hero of New-Orleans. Hudson, New York: William E. Norman, 1828.

"A Gentleman of the Baltimore Bar," *Some Account of General Jackson, Drawn up from the Hon. Mr. Eaton's very circumstantial narrative, and other well-established information respecting him.* Baltimore: Henry Vicary, 1828.

1832

PRENTICE, GEORGE DENISON. *Biography of Henry Clay.* Hartford, Connecticut: S. Henmer and J. J. Phelps, 1831.

GOODWIN, PHILO A. *Biography of Andrew Jackson, President of the United States, Formerly Major General in the Army of the United States.* Hartford: Clapp and Benton, 1832.

1836

HOLLAND, WILLIAM M. *The Life and Political Opinions of Martin Van Buren, Vice President of the United States.* Hartford: Belknap and Hamersley, 1835.

HALL, JAMES. *A Memoir of the Public Services of William Henry Harrison of Ohio.* Philadelphia: Edward C. Biddle, 1836.

A Sketch of the Life and Public Services of General William Henry Harrison, Candidate of the People for President of the United States. New Orleans: Young Men's Tippecanoe Association of New Orleans, 1840.

HILDRETH, RICHARD. *The People's Presidential Candidate; or the Life of William Henry Harrison of Ohio.* 4th ed. Boston: Weeks, Jordan and Company, 1840.

HILDRETH, RICHARD. *The Contrast: Or William Henry Harrison versus Martin Van Buren.* Boston: Weeks, Jordan and Company, 1840.

CUSHING, CALEB. *Outlines of the Life and Public Services, Civil and Military, of William Henry Harrison.* Boston: Weeks, Jordan and Company, 1840.

1844

[HICKMAN, G. H.?]. *The Life and Public Services of the Hon. James Knox Polk with a Compendium of His Speeches on Various Public Measures. Also a Sketch of the Life of the Hon. George Mifflin Dallas.* Baltimore: N. Hickman, 1844.

BROWNLOW, WILLIAM G. *A Political Register Setting Forth the Principles of the Whig and Locofoco Parties in the United States, with the Life and Public Services of Henry Clay.* Jonesborough, Tennessee: The Jonesborough *Whig,* 1844.

Life of John Tyler, President of the United States, up to the Close of the Second Session of the Twenty-Seventh Congress; Including some of his most important speeches while a member of the House of Representatives and of the Senate of the United States, and his principal messages and other public papers as Chief Magistrate of of the Union. New York: Harper and Brothers, 1844.

BANCROFT, GEORGE. *Martin Van Buren, To the End of His Career.* New York: Harper and Brothers, 1889 [written for campaign of 1844].

1848

Life of General Lewis Cass: Comprising an Account of His Military Services in the North-West during the War with Great Britain, His Diplomatic Career and Civil History, to Which is Appended a Sketch of the Public and Private History of Major-General W. O.

Butler of the Volunteer Service of the United States. Philadelphia: G. B. Zieber and Company, 1848.

Life and Public Services of Gen. Lewis Cass, Democratic Candidate for the Presidency, together with a Sketch of the Life and Services of Gen. William O. Butler, Democratic Candidate for the Vice-Presidency. Boston: J. B. Hall, 1848.

FRY, J. REESE, and ROBERT T. CONRAD. *A Life of Zachary Taylor; Comprising a Narrative of Events Connected with His Professional Career, Derived from Public Documents and Private Correspondence; and Authentic Incidents of His Early Years, from Materials Collected by Robert T. Conrad*. Philadelphia: Grigg, Elliot and Company, 1848.

1852

MANSFIELD, EDWARD D. *Life and Services of General Winfield Scott*. New York: A. S. Barnes, 1852.

HAWTHORNE, NATHANIEL. *Life of Franklin Pierce*. Boston: Ticknor, Reed and Fields, 1852.

BARTLETT, D. W. *The Life of Gen. Franklin Pierce, of New Hampshire, The Democratic Candidate for President of the United States*. Auburn, New York: Derby and Miller, 1852.

1856

BIGELOW, JOHN. *Memoir of the Life and Public Services of John Charles Frémont, Including an Account of His Explorations, Discoveries and Adventures on Five Successive Expeditions Across the North American Continent; Voluminous Selections from His Private and Public Correspondence; His Defence before the Court Martial, and Full Reports of His Principal Speeches in the Senate of the United States*. New York: Derby and Jackson, 1856.

HORTON, R. G. *The Life and Public Services of James Buchanan, Late Minister and Formerly Minister to Russia, Senator and Representative in Congress, and Secretary of State; Including the Most Important of His State Papers*. New York: Derby and Jackson, 1856.

1860

"A Member of the Western Bar," *Life of Stephen A. Douglas*. New York: Derby and Jackson, 1860.

SHEAHAN, JAMES W. *The Life of Stephen A. Douglas.* New York: Harper and Brothers, 1860.

BARTLETT, D. W. *The Life and Public Services of Abraham Lincoln.* New York: H. Dayton, 1860.

WASHBURNE, ELIHU B. *Abraham Lincoln: His Personal History and Public Record.* Washington: Republican Congressional Committee, 1860.

HOWELLS, WILLIAM DEAN. *Life of Abraham Lincoln.* Springfield, Illinois: Abraham Lincoln Association, 1938 [first published 1860].

1864

RAYMOND, HENRY J. *History of the Administration of President Lincoln, including his speeches, letters, addresses, proclamations, and messages; with a preliminary sketch of his life.* New York: Derby and Miller, 1864.

Life and Public Services of Abraham Lincoln, Sixteenth President of the United States, and Commander-in-Chief of the Army and Navy of the United States. Philadelphia: T. B. Peterson and Brothers, 1864.

THAYER, WILLIAM M. *The Character and Public Services of Abraham Lincoln, President of the United States.* Boston: Walker, Wise and Company, 1864.

The Life, Campaigns, and Public Services of General McClellan (George B. McClellan) the Hero of Western Virginia! South Mountain! and Antietam! Philadelphia: T. B. Peterson and Brothers, 1864.

1868

DEMING, HENRY C. *The Life of Ulysses S. Grant, General United States Army.* Hartford: S. S. Scranton and Company, 1868.

OPTIC, OLIVER [pseudonym, W. T. Adams]. *Our Standard-Bearer; or, the Life of General Ulysses S. Grant: His Youth, His Manhood, His Campaigns, and His Eminent Services in the Reconstruction of the Nation His Sword Has Redeemed: As Seen and Related by Captain Bernard Galligasken, Cosmopolitan, and Written out by Oliver Optic.* Boston: Lee and Shepard, 1868.

CROLY, DAVID G. *Seymour and Blair; Their Lives and Services with an Appendix Containing a History of Reconstruction.* New York: Richardson and Company, 1868.

MCCABE, JAMES D., JR. *Life and Public Services of Horatio Seymour and . . . Francis P. Blair, Jr.* New York: United States Publishing Company, 1868.

1872

GREELEY, HORACE. *The Autobiography of Horace Greeley.* New York: E. B. Treat, 1872.

REAVIS, L. U. *A Representative Life of Horace Greeley.* New York: G. W. Carleton and Company, 1872.

CHAMBERLAIN, EVERETT. *The Struggle of '72* [Ulysses S. Grant]. Chicago: Union Publishing Company, 1872.

1876

CONWELL, RUSSELL HERMAN. *Life and Public Services of Gov. Rutherford B. Hayes.* Boston: B. B. Russell, 1876.

HOWELLS, WILLIAM DEAN. *Sketch of the Life and Character of Rutherford B. Hayes: Also a Biographical Sketch of William A. Wheeler, with Portraits of Both Candidates.* Boston: H. O. Houghton and Company, 1876.

COOK, THEODORE P. *The Life and Public Services of Hon. Samuel J. Tilden, Democratic Nominee for President of the United States. To Which is added a Sketch of the Life of Hon. Thomas A. Hendricks, Democratic Nominee for Vice-President.* New York: D. Appleton and Company, 1876.

1880

BRISBIN, GENERAL JAMES S. *From the Tow-Path to the White House: The Early Life and Public Career of James A. Garfield, Maj. General, U. S. A. The spicy record of a wonderful career which, like that of Abraham Lincoln, by native energy and untiring industry, led this man from obscurity to the foremost position in the councils of the nation. Including also a sketch of the life of Hon. Chester A. Arthur.* Philadelphia: Hubbard Brothers, 1880.

FORNEY, JOHN W. *Life and Military Career of Winfield Scott Hancock. This Work Comprises His Early Life, Education and Remarkable Military Career, which has made him Senior Major General of the Armies of the United States, and the Choice of the Democracy of the Nation for the High Office of President. It also contains a succinct Biographical Sketch of Hon. William H. English.* Philadelphia: Hubbard Brothers, 1880.

Conwell, Russell Herman. *The Life, Speeches, and Public Services of Gen. James A. Garfield.* Boston: B. B. Russell, 1880.

1884

Boutwell, George S. *Why I Am a Republican: A History of the Republican Party, A Defense of Its Policy, and the Reasons Which Justify Its Continuance in Power, with Biographical Sketches of the Republican Candidates* [James G. Blaine]. Hartford: William J. Betts and Company, 1884.

Conwell, Russell Herman. *The Life and Public Services of James G. Blaine, with Incidents, Anecdotes, and Romantic Events Connected with His Early Life; Containing also His Speeches and Important Historical Documents Relating to His Later Years.* Augusta, Maine: E. C. Allen and Company, 1884.

LaFevre, General Benjamin. *Biographies of S. Grover Cleveland, the Democratic Candidate for President, and Thomas A. Hendricks, the Democratic Candidate for Vice-President, with a Description of the Leading Issues and the Proceedings of the National Convention, together with a History of the Political Parties of the United States; Comparisons of Platforms on all Important Questions, and Political Tables for Ready Reference.* Chicago: Baird and Dillon, 1884.

1888

Hensel, William Uhler, assisted by George F. Parker. *Life and Public Services of Grover Cleveland, Twenty-Second President of the United States and Democratic Nominee for Re-election, 1888.* Philadelphia: Hubbard Brothers, 1888.

Northrop, Henry Davenport. *The Life and Public Services of Gen. Benj. Harrison, as a Man the Noblest and Purest of His Times; as a Citizen, the Grandest of His Nation; as a Statesman, Idol of Millions of People: The Great American Statesman. Embracing a Full Account of His Early Life; His Ambition as a Student; His Able and Patriotic Record as a Soldier; His Honorable Career as a Senator, etc., etc., to which is added the Life and Public Services of Hon. Lewis P. Morton.* Philadelphia: International Publishing Company, 1888.

Wallace, General Lew. *Life of Gen. Ben Harrison; also Life of Hon. Levi P. Morton, by George Alfred Townsend (Gath.).* Philadelphia: Hubbard Brothers, 1888.

1892

CAMPBELL-COPELAND, THOMAS (ed. and comp.). *Cleveland and Stevenson; Their Lives and Record*. New York: Charles L. Webster and Company, 1892.

PARKER, GEORGE F. *A Life of Grover Cleveland*. New York: Cassell Publishing Co., 1892.

1896

METCALF, RICHARD L. *Life and Patriotic Services of Hon. William J. Bryan, the fearless and Brilliant Leader of the People and Candidate for President of the United States; A Sketch from the Beginning of His Career to the High Position He Holds in the Affection of His Countrymen—an Affection Won by His Devotion and Loyalty to the Welfare of the Toiling Masses of America; also, the Life of Hon. Arthur Sewall, Candidate for Vice-President, together with Many Interesting Articles Bearing on the Great Issue of the Day*. N.P.: Edgewood Publishing Company, 1896.

OGILVIE, J. S. (ed.). *Life and Speeches of William McKinley, Containing a Sketch of His Eventful Life—A Collection of His Best and Most Thrilling Speeches—Proceedings of the National Convention, St. Louis—Platform of the Republican Party—Sketch of the Candidate for Vice-President—and Other Valuable Information for Every Citizen* (with an introduction by Hon. Stewart L. Woodford). New York: J. S. Ogilvie Publishing Company, 1896.

PORTER, ROBERT P. *Life of William McKinley, Soldier, Lawyer, Statesman*. Cleveland: N. G. Hamilton, 1896.

1900

NEWBRANCH, HARVEY E. *William Jennings Bryan: A Concise but Complete Story of His Life and Services*. Lincoln, Nebraska: The University Publishing Company, 1900.

DOS PASSOS, JOHN R. *Defence of the McKinley Administration*. New York: J. R. Dos Passos, 1900.

HALSTEAD, MURAT. *Victorious Republicanism and lives of the standard bearers, McKinley and Roosevelt*. [Chicago?]: Republican National Publishing Co., 1900.

1904

GRADY, COLONEL JOHN R. *The Lives and Public Services of Parker and Davis*. Philadelphia: Elliott Publishing Company, 1904.

Riis, Jacob A. *Theodore Roosevelt the Citizen.* New York: The Outlook Company, 1904.

Andrews, Byron. *The Facts about the Candidate* [Theodore Roosevelt]. Chicago: Sam Stone, 1904.

1908

Davis, Oscar King. *William Howard Taft, The Man of the Hour: His Biography and His Views on the Great Questions of To-day.* (Including a chapter by Theodore Roosevelt, President of the United States.) Philadelphia: P. W. Ziegler Company, 1908.

Gale, Albert L., and George W. Kline. *Bryan the Man: The Great Commoner at Close Range: An Intimate and Impartial Review of the Personal Side of His Public Career.* St. Louis: The Thompson Publishing Company, 1908.

1912

Hosford, Hester E. *Woodrow Wilson and New Jersey Made Over.* New York: G. P. Putnam's Sons, 1912.

Hale, W. B. *Woodrow Wilson: The Story of His Life.* New York: Doubleday, 1912.

Walker, Albert H. *The Administration of William H. Taft.* New York: Albert H. Walker, 1912.

1916

Ford, Henry Jones. *Woodrow Wilson, the Man and His Work.* New York: D. Appleton and Company, 1916.

Ransom, William L. *Charles E. Hughes: The Statesman as Shown in the Opinions of the Jurist.* New York: E. P. Dutton and Company, 1916.

1920

Babson, Roger W. *Cox—the Man.* New York: Brentano's, 1920.

Morris, Charles E. *Progressive Democracy of James M. Cox.* Indianapolis: Bobbs-Merrill, 1920.

Schortemeier, Frederick E. *Rededicating America: Life and Recent Speeches of Warren G. Harding.* Indianapolis: Bobbs-Merrill, 1920.

Chapple, J. M. *Warren G. Harding—the Man.* Boston: Chapple Publishing Company, 1920.

1924

WOODS, ROBERT ARCHERY. *The Preparation of Calvin Coolidge: An Interpretation.* Boston: Houghton Mifflin Company, 1924.

HUNTLEY, THEODORE A. *The Life of John W. Davis.* New York: Duffield Company, 1924.

ROBERTS, KENNETH L. *Concentrated New England: a Sketch of Calvin Coolidge.* Indianapolis: Bobbs-Merrill, 1924.

1928

ROOSEVELT, FRANKLIN D. *The Happy Warrior, Alfred E. Smith, A Study of a Public Servant.* Boston: Houghton Mifflin, 1928.

HAPGOOD, N., and HENRY MOSKOWITZ. *Up from the City Streets* [Alfred E. Smith]. New York: Harcourt, 1927.

IRWIN, WILL. *Herbert Hoover: A Reminiscent Biography.* New York: The Century Company, 1928.

1932

DEXTER, WALTER FRIAR. *Herbert Hoover and American Individualism: A Modern Interpretation of a National Ideal.* New York: The Macmillan Company, 1932.

ROSS, LELAND M., and ALLEN W. GROBIN. *This Democratic Roosevelt, The Life Story of "F.D."; An Authentic Biography.* New York: E. P. Dutton, 1932.

LINDLEY, ERNEST K. *Franklin D. Roosevelt: A Career in Progressive Democracy.* New York: Blue Ribbon Books, 1932.

1936

THORNTON, WILLIS. *The Life of Alfred M. Landon.* New York: Grosset and Dunlap, 1936.

FOWLER, RICHARD B. *Deeds Not Deficits: The Story of Alfred M. Landon* (with an introduction by William Allen White). N.P.: n.d.

BRANDEIS, E. *Franklin D. Roosevelt, the Man.* New York: American Offset Corporation, 1936.

1940

WALKER, STANLEY. *This Is Wendell Willkie.* New York: Dodd, Mead and Company, 1940.

MAKEY, H. O. *Wendell Willkie of Elwood.* Elwood, Indiana: National Book Company, 1940.

156

LUDWIG, EMIL. *Roosevelt.* New York: Garden City Publishing Company, 1940.

1944

WALKER, STANLEY. *Dewey, An American of This Century.* New York: McGraw-Hill, 1944.

HUGHES, RUPERT. *Story of Thomas E. Dewey, Attorney for the People.* New York: Grosset, 1944.

1948

MCNAUGHTON, FRANK, and WALTER HEHMEYER. *Harry Truman.* New York: McGraw-Hill, 1948.

SCHAUFFLER, E. R. *Harry Truman, Son of the Soil.* Kansas City: E. R. Schauffler, 1948.

1952

GUNTHER, JOHN. *Eisenhower, The Man and The Symbol.* New York: Harper and Brothers, 1952.

MCCANN, KEVIN. *Man from Abilene* [Dwight D. Eisenhower]. New York: Doubleday, 1952.

DAVIS, KENNETH S. *Soldier of Democracy* [Dwight D. Eisenhower]. New York: Doubleday, 1952.

BUSCH, NOEL F. *Adlai E. Stevenson of Illinois.* New York: Farrar, Straus and Young, 1952.

MARTIN, JOHN BARTLOW. *Adlai Stevenson.* New York: Harper and Brothers, 1952.

1956

PUSEY, M. J. *Eisenhower the President.* New York: Macmillan, 1956.

DONOVAN, R. J. *Eisenhower; the Inside Story.* New York: Harper and Brothers, 1956.

IVES, E. S. *My Brother Adlai.* New York: Morrow, 1956.

1960

AMRINE, MICHAEL. *This is Humphrey.* New York: Doubleday, 1960.

BURNS, JAMES M. *John Kennedy: A Political Profile.* New York: Harcourt, Brace, 1960.

MACCARTHY, JOE. *The Remarkable Kennedys.* New York: Dial, 1960.

157

MANCHESTER, WILLIAM. *A Rockefeller Family Portrait*. New York: Little, Brown, 1959.

MAZO, EARL. *Richard Nixon*. New York: Harper and Brothers, 1959.

MORRIS, JOE ALEX. *Nelson Rockefeller*. New York: Harper and Brothers, 1960.

POLING, JAMES, ed. *Rockefeller Speaks*. New York: Crowell, 1960.

WELLMAN, PAUL I. *Stuart Symington: Portrait of a Man With a Mission*. New York: Doubleday, 1960.

A BIBLIOGRAPHICAL ESSAY

Part of the task undertaken in this study was to relate the ideas and ideals found in the campaign biographies to ideas and ideals contemporary with them in American society. This would have been relatively simple if there had existed a body of historical scholarship which traced the evolution of each of the ideas and ideals that have been encountered. Happily, there are a number of these themes which have received able scholarly attention. The "agrarian myth" and the "cult of success" are excellent examples of ideas whose development and implication have been dealt with in a highly competent body of scholarly literature. There are other themes, however, on which relatively little scholarly work has been done. The evolving concept of the ideal mother and father and the ideal of boyhood are outstanding illustrations. Still other themes fall in-between.

Patently, every major theme encountered in the campaign lives is a subject of such magnitude as to require extended scholarly investigation. Thus the case of those themes which have not received much in the way of scholarly attention posed a real dilemma. They could not properly be related to ideas contemporary with them without full-scale original investigation to determine their development and implication in American society as a whole. Frankly, this was not done. Had it been done, the results would have had to be presented in a separate volume or volumes to do the subjects justice. Yet it was equally unthinkable simply to abandon as hopeless the task of relating them to their cultural context. Compromise, admittedly too frequently a euphemism for mutual disappointment, resulted. Original investigation was undertaken—obviously not deep or complete enough to fill the void in scholarship, but enough to indicate possible lines for future investigators and, more importantly here, enough, it is hoped, to make the generalizations at least tenable.

The following essay on the sources is offered with the above observations in mind. It does not pretend to be an exhaustive bibliography on each of the themes encountered in the biographies. Its function, rather, is to present, on the themes where the scholarly path is well beaten, the best treatments of the theme. Nearly all of these works contain extensive bibliographies. It would serve no useful purpose to reproduce them. Where the scholarly path wanders, taking the investigator through many fragmentary treatments and much that is tangential to the theme, the works cited represent merely those that have proved most useful in piecing together the development of the theme.

Introduction

The quoted material relative to the symbolic nature of the Presidency is from Sidney Hyman, *The American President* (New York, 1954), 11–12.

Chapter 1. Heralds of Destiny: On the Making of Campaign Biographies

Needless to say, the literature on the conduct of presidential campaigns is extensive. Yet no one has previously concerned himself with the problem of how campaign biographies in general come to be written. The sources cited below represent merely those which proved helpful in ferreting out an answer.

The most substantial body of published primary material concerning the affairs of the major parties are their official reports: *Official Report of the Proceedings of the Democratic National Convention, 1832–1956;* and *Official Report of the Republican National Convention, 1856–1956.* For the very meager unpublished material, see an excellent article by Donald R. McCoy, "The Records of the Democratic and Republican National Committees," *The American Archivist,* XIV (October, 1951), 313–21, which furnishes a detailed survey of all types of records retained by the parties.

Of the fairly numerous politicians who have divulged "trade secrets," the most useful in this connection were James A. Farley, *Behind the Ballots, The Personal History of a Politician* (New York, 1938); Charles Michelson, *The Ghost Talks* (New York, 1944); John W. Forney, *Anecdotes of Public Men* (2 vols., New York, 1873–1881); John Bigelow, *Retrospections of an Active Life* (5 vols., New York, 1909–1913); and George F. Parker, *Recollections of Grover Cleveland* (New York, 1911).

The published correspondence of candidates was severely disappointing. Only the Hayes letters (Charles R. Williams [ed.], *Diary and Letters of Rutherford B. Hayes* [5 vols., Columbus, Ohio, 1922–

26]) held any substantial information about campaign biographies. The Lincoln correspondence (Roy P. Basler [ed.], *Collected Works of Abraham Lincoln* [8 vols., New Brunswick, 1953]) was also useful and, to a lesser extent, so were the letters of Jackson (John Spencer Basset [ed.], *Correspondence of Andrew Jackson* [7 vols., Washington 1926–1935]). Considerably more material was found among the unpublished papers of Benjamin Harrison in the Library of Congress. Few campaign biographers have attained the eminence of having their papers collected. The correspondence of William Dean Howells, a notable exception, proved useful (Mildred Howells [ed.], *Life in Letters of William Dean Howells* [2 vols., New York, 1928]). Hawthorne as a campaign biographer is treated briefly in Randall Stewart's admirable *Nathaniel Hawthorne, A Biography* (New Haven, 1948).

The author corresponded with a number of campaign biographers and the publishing houses that brought out their work. Both authors and publishers proved very helpful. Especial gratitude is due Stanley Walker and Noel F. Busch, and Harper & Brothers, Dodd, Mead, McGraw-Hill, Doubleday, Houghton Mifflin, E. P. Dutton, and Farrar, Straus & Young. Former chairmen of the Democratic and Republican national committees Stephen A. Mitchell and Leonard W. Hall were similarly helpful.

For the material on the campaign biographies of Lincoln, see a unique and admirable study by Ernest J. Wessen, "Campaign Lives of Abraham Lincoln," *Papers in Illinois History . . . 1937* (Springfield, 1938).

Chapter 2. Ancestors: The Blood of Heroes

One of the most delightful books in the field of American social history is Dixon Wecter, *The Saga of American Society: A Record of Social Aspirations, 1607–1937* (New York, 1937). It is the only book-length historical treatment of the subject of ancestor worship and aristocratic pretensions in American society. Wallace E. Davies, *Patriotism on Parade: The Story of Veterans' and Hereditary Organizations in America, 1783–1900* (Cambridge, 1955) is very useful for hereditary organizations.

For the early period Louise B. Dunbar, *A Study of "Monarchial" Tendencies in the U. S. from 1776 to 1801* (Urbana, 1922), provides a good discussion of the proposals for the establishment of a monarchy and also a discussion of the controversy concerning the Order of the Cincinnati. On the latter, Davies, *Patriotism on*

Parade provides not only an excellent coverage but also a complete guide to the monographic material on the subject. For two views on early aristocratic pretensions see Rufus W. Griswold, *The Republican Court or American Society in the Days of Washington* (New York, 1855), and Edgar S. Maclay (ed.), *The Journal of William Maclay* (New York, 1927). For the effect of the great revolutionary upheavals, see J. Franklin Jameson, *The American Revolution Considered as a Social Movement* (Princeton, 1926), and Charles D. Hazen, *Contemporary American Opinion of the French Revolution* (Baltimore, 1897). It is, of course, impossible to do justice to the literature that deals with the degree to which men and movements in the early history of the Republic were aristocratic or democratic. Almost every work concerned with the pre-Civil War period touches upon this controversy at some point.

The custom of bestowing "republican titles" has aroused continuous remark by both home-grown and foreign commentators. For an early newspaper denunciation of the custom as "of monarchial origin and absurd in a republic," see "Mirabeau," "Forerunners of Monarchy and Aristocracy in the United States," *National Gazette*, December 12, 1792. A magazine writer felt that they were only necessary "when the people are sunk into depravity," *American Museum*, XI (March, 1792), 86. At mid-century Horace Greeley, cooling his heels in a French jail, reflected philosophically on this trait in his countrymen. See L. U. Reavis, *A Representative Life of Horace Greeley* (New York, 1872), 120, wherein Greeley's meditations are quoted at length. Foreign traveler Alexander Mackay noticed it in the 1840's in *The Western World; or Travels in the United States in 1846–47* (2 vols., Philadelphia, 1849). And at the end of the century it was commented upon by Lord Bryce, *The American Commonwealth* (2 vols., 3d ed., New York, 1897). Henry Steele Commager has noted this phenomenon briefly in *The American Mind: An Interpretation of American Thought and Character Since the 1880's* (New Haven, 1950).

For some of the other trappings of caste, see Franklin B. Dexter, "On Some Social Distinctions at Harvard and Yale Before the Revolution," *Proceedings of the American Antiquarian Society*, new series, IX (October, 1893), 34–59; see the *Boston Magazine*, I (February, 1784), 164, for a good description of a public procession; see also "On the Dresses of Judges," *American Museum*, XII (August, 1792), 83–84.

For an appreciation of the adroitness of the campaign biographer in fashioning the candidate's ancestors to correspond with the school-book image of the heroes of the Republic, several pioneer studies of American textbooks are indispensable. Richard D. Mosier, *Making the American Mind: Social and Moral Ideas in the McGuffy Readers* (New York, 1947) ; Vincent A. Davis, *The Literature of Advanced School Readers in the United States, 1785–1900* (Chicago, 1937) ; and Bessie Louise Pierce, *Civic Attitudes In American School Textbooks* (Chicago, 1930). These three works, and especially Mosier and Pierce, have been used throughout this study. It is a great disadvantage to the student of ideas in America that schoolbooks as vehicles of ideas have not received as much scholarly attention as they deserve.

Chapter 3. Parents: The Hand That Rocked the Cradle

The only extensive work dealing with the history of the American family is the pioneering *Social History of the American Family from Colonial Times to the Present* published by Arthur W. Calhoun in 1918 (3 vols., Cleveland). Considering the extreme paucity of monographic studies available to him, Calhoun's work is a remarkable achievement. (Particularly impressive is his utilization of a considerable body of the writings of foreign travelers.) Now, forty years later, the situation has not changed much. A striking illustration of the neglect of the history of the American family by social historians is afforded by the volumes in the *History of American Life* series, especially the two volumes that cover the period 1790–1850: John A. Krout and Dixon R. Fox, *The Completion of Independence, 1790–1830* (New York, 1944), and Carl R. Fish, *The Rise of the Common Man, 1830–1850* (New York, 1927).

Three studies must be excepted from this blanket indictment: Edmund S. Morgan, *The Puritan Family: Essays on Religion and Domestic Relations in Seventeenth-Century New England* (Boston, 1944) ; Edmund S. Morgan, *Virginians at Home: Family Life in the Eighteenth Century* (Williamsburg, 1952) ; and Anne L. Kuhn, *The Mother's Role in Childhood Education: New England Concepts, 1830–1860* (New Haven, 1947).

There is an extensive literature dealing with the role of women in American life. Much of the best of it, from the point of view of the historian of ideas, is by scholars in American literature. The most recent is William Wasserstrom, *Heiress of All the Ages* (Minneapolis, 1959) which provides an excellent bibliographical coverage in its notes.

Sociologists have, of course, labored mightily in this field, but their approach, even when they concern themselves with the evolution of the family as an institution, does not fill this void. Having their own orientation, methodology, and objectives, they do not pretend to be writing history. See, for example, the excellent little volume by John Sirjamaki, *The American Family in the Twentieth Century* (Cambridge, 1953), in the Library of Congress series in American Civilization.

Chapter 4. How Dear to My Heart: Swimmin' Hole to Playing Field

The evolution of childhood from the early children-should-be-seen-and-not-heard norm to the mischievous, fun-loving boy has not in itself formed a subject for serious historical treatment. Most of the works cited in connection with Chapter III contain much that is relevant. See also Sandford Fleming, *Children and Puritanism* (New Haven, 1933).

Probably the nearest approach to this theme is made in several books that deal with children's literature. Outstanding among these are Monica Kiefer, *American Children Through Their Books, 1700–1835* (Philadelphia, 1948); and William Sloane, *Children's Books in England & America in the Seventeenth Century* (New York, 1955). Also useful are Elva S. Smith, *The History of Children's Literature* (Chicago, 1937); and Cornelia Meigs et al., *A Critical History of Children's Literature* (New York, 1953). There are several studies of individual writers of juvenile fiction that contributed to the development of this theme: Herbert R. Mayes, *Alger: A Biography Without a Hero* (New York, 1928); and John L. Cutler, *Gilbert Patten and His Frank Merriwell Saga: A Study in Sub-Literary Fiction, 1896–1913* (Orono, Maine, 1934). The studies of schoolbooks, cited in Chapter II, should not be ignored in this connection.

Henry Steele Commager presents a brief but incisive picture of boyhood in the nineteenth century in his *American Mind* and a charming essay on juvenile fiction, anthologized in the *Saturday Review Reader, No. 2* (New York, 1953).

For examples of early comment on the "cult" of childhood from the nation's periodical press, see "Morality in Childhood," *The Knickerbocker or New-York Monthly Magazine*, VIII (December, 1836), 676–77; "Charles Civil" [a letter to the editor and the editor's reply], *The Literary Magazine and American Register*, IV (October, 1805), 289–91; "Aristippus," "Modern Manners," *North American Review*, I (May, 1815), 19–21; "Tacita," "Defective Education," *Ladies Repository*, I (September, 1841), 258. For dire prophecy in a book-length treatment, see *The Victim of Indulgence: By a Teacher of Youth Founded on Fact* (Boston, 1832).

The files of the *Youth's Companion* and *St. Nicholas,* best of the many juvenile magazines, are indispensable.

For the development of American ideas concerning the value of athletics, the principal reliance has been upon the *History of American Life* series. The kind of summary statement that these volumes were obliged to make proved to be ideal for the purpose intended here. Particular attention should be called, however, to several works that furnish excellent insights into the reciprocal impact that sport and the conditions of American life have had on each other. In this respect see especially John A. Krout, *Annals of American Sport* (New Haven, 1929); John R. Betts, "The Technological Revolution and the Rise of Sport, 1850–1900," *Mississippi Valley Historical Review,* XL (September, 1953), 231–56.

Chapter 5. Making His Way: Life Is Real; Life Is Earnest

Almost every history of education in the United States, and there have been many, deals to some extent with the values that have been popularly supposed to result from education. For the idea that it was believed vital for the preservation of the Republic by the Founding Fathers, see, for example, Elwood P. Cubberly, *Public Education in the United States* (rev. ed., Boston, 1934) and Stuart G. Noble, *A History of American Education* (rev. ed., New York, 1954). That this idea has been repeated ad infinitum by lesser politicians, state legislatures, and other public bodies has been thoroughly documented by Edgar W. Knight in *A Documentary History of Education in the South before 1860* (5 vols., Chapel Hill, 1949–1954).

While both Cubberly and Noble give some attention to a host of other reasons advanced to support the cause of public education, a more detailed account can, quite naturally, be found in works that are restricted to this subject. Especially good are Merle Curti, *Social Ideas of American Educators* (New York, 1935) and George S. Counts, *The Social Foundations of Education* (New York, 1934) quoted in the text. Useful also in this connection are Lawrence A. Cremin, *The American Common School; An Historic Conception* (New York, 1951) and Philip R. V. Curoe, *Educational Attitudes of Organized Labor in the United States* (New York, 1926).

In his *Growth of American Thought*, Merle Curti has an excellent summary of the American passion for "self-improvement," furnishing abundant evidence on the same attitude discovered in the campaign biographies concerning self-education as a means of making up deficiency in formal schooling, rather than an alternative to be preferred to formal schooling.

There is, as yet, no full-length historical treatment of anti-intellectualism in the United States. While there is a vast literature dealing with various phases of life in America in which anti-intellectual patterns of thought occur, most of it is not historical. Altogether the most satisfactory brief treatment is Merle Curti, "Intellectuals and Other People," *American Historical Review*, XLV (January, 1955), 18–47. The notes to this article furnish as good a bibliography as is available on the subject. Part of the difficulty of ferreting out the work that has been done on anti-intellectualism is the amorphous nature of the term. Much material is available in the already large and rapidly growing body of literature in mass communication and mass culture that Curti has not included. For a sizable introduction to this material, see Bernard Rosenberg and David Manning White, *Mass Culture: The Popular Arts in America* (Glencoe, Ill., 1957) and the bibliographies therein.

The most recent extensive treatment of the cult of success is Irvin G. Wyllie, *The Self-Made Man in America: The Myth of Rags to Riches* (New Brunswick, 1954). This admirable work, while primarily a study of nineteenth-century success books, provides an excellent summary of the scholarship on this subject. Excellent brief discussions are contained in Curti, *Growth of American Thought* and Ralph Henry Gabriel, *The Course of American Democratic Thought: An Intellectual History Since 1815* (New York, 1940). See also Marshall W. Fishwick, *American Heroes: Myth and Reality* (Washington, 1954), Chapter X.

For the European background—the "Protestant ethic"—the standard works are Richard Tawney, *Religion and the Rise of Capitalism* (New York, 1926); Max Weber, *The Protestant Ethic and the Spirit of Capitalism* (New York, 1930); and Ernst Troeltsch, *Protestantism and Progress, A Historical Study of the Relation of Protestantism to the Modern World* (New York, 1912). Specifically for the English background, see Louis B. Wright, *Middle Class Culture in Elizabethan England* (Chapel Hill, 1935).

For the early American nurture of the cult of success, see Alfred W. Griswold, "Three Puritans on Prosperity," *New England Quarterly*, VII (September, 1934), 475–93; Louis B. Wright, "Franklin's Legacy to the Gilded Age," *Virginia Quarterly Review*, XXII (Spring, 1946), 268–79; Dixon Wecter, *The Hero in America: A Chronicle of Hero Worship* (New York, 1941), Chapter IV.

For the more recent period, in addition to Wyllie, *Self-Made Man in America*, see also A. Whitney Griswold, "New Thought: A Cult of Success," *American Journal of Sociology*, XLC (November, 1934), 309–18.

Chapter 6. An Interlude of Martial Glory

World War II and the decade of "cold war" that has followed have brought with them a new interest in the professional soldier, the militia tradition, and the whole problem of standing armies in time of "peace." A spate of good books has grown out of this new concern. All of them address themselves, in some measure, to the task of tracing the history of the American prejudices against standing armies and in favor of citizen-soldiers. Especially noteworthy are: Samuel P. Huntington, *The Soldier and the State* (Cambridge, 1957); Arthur A. Ekirch, Jr., *The Civilian and the Military* (New York, 1956); Joseph Bernardo and Eugene H. Bacon, *American Military Policy: Its Development Since 1775* (Harrisburg, Pa., 1955); and Louis Smith, *American Democracy and Military Power: A Study of Civil Control of the Military Power in the United States* (Chicago, 1951). The first three titles contain extensive bibliographies, providing, among them, as complete a coverage of the literature on this subject as is available.

Dorothy B. and Julius Goebel, *Generals in the White House* (New York, 1952) provides a brief but cogent summary of the ideas discussed in this chapter. Additional aspects of the role of the military hero in American politics are treated in P. F. Boller, Jr., "Professional Soldiers in the White House," *Southwest Review*, XXXVII (Autumn, 1952), 269–79; Albert Somit, "The Military Hero as Presidential Candidate," *Public Opinion Quarterly*, XII (Summer, 1948), 192–200; L. B. Wheilcon, "Military Leaders and the Presidency," *Editorial Research Reports* (December 5, 1947), 869–83; and Frank Weitenkampf, "Generals in Politics," *American Scholar*, XIII (Summer, 1944), 375–78.

For the English background of the prejudice, see J. S. Omond, *Parliament and the Army, 1632–1904* (London, 1933). Material on the American constitutional struggle is from Charles Warren, *The Making of the Constitution* (Boston, 1938); Irving Brant, *James Madison, Father of the Constitution* (Indianapolis, 1950); and Johnathan Elliot (comp.), *The Debates in the Several State Conventions on the Adoption of the Federal Constitution* (4 vols., 2d ed., Washington, 1836).

For early pronouncements of this belief in the militia from the pulpit, see Merle Curti, *The Roots of American Loyalty* (New York, 1946). For an able discussion of the myths fostered by the battle of New Orleans, see John William Ward, *Andrew Jackson: Symbol for an Age* (New York, 1955). For the persistence of the belief in the superiority of the citizen-soldier during the Civil War, see T. Harry Williams, "The Attack Upon West Point During the Civil War," *Mississippi Valley Historical Review*, XXV (March, 1939), 491–504. For the contribution of school texts to the continuance of this belief, see Bessie Louise Pierce, *Civic Attitudes in American School Textbooks* (Chicago, 1930). The McGuffey readers, "more than any other readers of the same period," were strong in their denunciations of war and militarism, yet they, too, glorified American military heroes. See Mosier, *Making of the American Mind*. Finally, no one interested in the ideas dealt with in this chapter should neglect what is probably the oldest classic on the subject—the trenchant indictment of Emory Upton, *The Military Policy of the United States* (Washington, 1907).

The final quoted summation is from Pendleton Herring, *The Impact of War: Our Democracy Under Arms* (New York, 1941).

Chapter 7. Cincinnatus Called from the Plow

For the past twenty years there has been a slow but steadily growing body of scholarship on the agrarian myth. The most recent summary may be found in Chapter I, "The Agrarian Myth and Commercial Realities," of Richard Hofstadter, *The Age of Reform: From Bryan to F. D. R.* (New York, 1955). This is an able and perceptive essay which not only embraces the entire body of important scholarship on the agrarian myth but also makes important contributions of its own. The notes to that chapter provide the best bibliography available on this subject. In the preparation of this chapter on the candidate as farmer, the pertinent portion of this literature was consulted. It is listed at length in an article by the author entitled, "The Cincinnatus Image in Presidential Politics," *Agricultural History*, XXI (April, 1957), 23–29.

For the European background of American agrarian thought, see Paul H. Johnstone, "In Praise of Husbandry," *Agricultural History*, XI (April, 1937), 80–95, and the same author's "Turnips and Romanticism," *Agricultural History*, XII (July, 1938) 224–55.

For the promotional literature during colonization see Chester E. Eisinger, "Land and Loyalty: Literary Expression of Agrarian Nationalism in the Seventeenth and Eighteenth Centuries," *American Literature*, XXI (May, 1949), 160–78. Eisinger treats the reinforcement of this belief in the Revolutionary period in "The Freehold Concept in Eighteenth-Century American Letters," *William and Mary Quarterly*, IV (January, 1947), 42–59. See also, by the same author, "The Farmer in the Eighteenth-Century Almanac," *Agricultural History*, XXVII (July, 1954), 107–12.

For Jefferson and the yeomanry, see A. Whitney Griswold, "The Agrarian Democracy of Thomas Jefferson," *American Political Science Review*, XL (August, 1946), 657–81, and Griswold, *Farming and Democracy* (New York, 1948), Chapter II.

For the progress of the agrarian myth across the continent, see Henry Nash Smith, *Virgin Land: The American West as Symbol and Myth* (Cambridge, 1950); especially pertinent is Book Three, "The Garden of the World." For the continued operation of the myth on the modern American mind, see Griswold, *Farming and Democracy*, Chapter V, and Hofstadter, *Age of Reform*, Chapter I.

Chapter 8. From the Law to the Market Place

No researcher need complain of a dearth of material relative to the legal profession. In keeping with the enduring reputation of the profession for verbosity, there is a monumental pile of evidence, gathered by four hundred researchers and published in 175 separate reports, representing the American Bar Association's Survey of the Legal Profession. This has been condensed for less hardy citizens in Albert P. Blaustein *et al.*, *The American Lawyer: A Summary of the Survey of the Legal Profession* (Chicago, 1954).

For historical treatment of the prejudice against lawyers, the best survey is still Charles Warren, *A History of the American Bar* (Boston, 1911). For a wider-ranging survey, see Roscoe Pound, *The Laywer from Antiquity to Modern Times, with Particular Reference to the Development of Bar Associations in the United States* (St. Paul, 1953). Also useful are: William Seagle, *The Quest for Law* (New York, 1941); James Willard Hurst, *The Growth of American Law: The Law Makers* (Boston, 1950); Roscoe Pound, "The Legal Profession in America," *Notre Dame Lawyer*, XIX (June, 1944), 334–54.

For the position that the American attitude toward lawyers has always been an ambivalent one, rather than an attitude marked by mysterious and violent changes, see Hurst, *Growth of American Law*. A more thorough and ably documented statement of this position is

Philip F. Detweiler, "Early American Lawyers and the Public," un-published paper, read before the Southern Historical Association on October 14, 1953, and reported in LeRoy R. Graf, "The Nineteenth Annual Meeting," *Journal of Southern History*, XX (February, 1954), 75.

The qualities that go to make up the businessman have also received their share of scholarly attention. It would be neither easy nor desirable to attempt to distinguish this literature from the literature already discussed in connection with the cult of success. Most of that literature is pertinent here also. Particularly is this true of works like Irvin Wyllie's *Self-Made Man in America*. Among the recent studies devoted to the realities rather than the myths of business success are William Miller (ed.), *Men in Business: Essays in the History of Entrepreneurship* (Cambridge, 1952) and Mabel Newcomer, *The Big Business Executive: The Factors that Made Him, 1900–1950* (New York, 1955). The bibliographies in these works cover adequately the literature on this aspect of the subject.

There are, however, some additional titles that have, perhaps, a more direct pertinence to the attempt made in this chapter to see the American businessman as a culture hero. There is some provocative material in James T. Adams, *Our Business Civilization: Some Aspects of American Culture* (New York, 1930) and in Thurman W. Arnold, *The Folklore of Capitalism* (New Haven, 1937). Miriam Beard, *A History of the Business Man* (New York, 1938) furnishes the necessary broad perspective.

A brief attempt to assess the place that business, the businessman, and business ideas occupied in the mind of the nation is made in Thomas C. Cochran and William Miller, *The Age of Enterprise: A Social History of Industrial America* (New York, 1949). A pioneer attempt to trace public opinion of the businessman historically by an examination of press reaction to the death of a select company of outstanding entrepreneurs from Stephen Girard to Henry Ford is Sigmund Diamond, *The Reputation of the American Businessman* (Cambridge, 1955). Three new studies that focus on the thought and motivation of the business mind and hence contribute to an understanding of the businessman as a culture hero are Robert G. McCloskey, *American Conservatism in the Age of Enterprise* (Cambridge, 1951); James W. Prothro, *Dollar Decade: Business Ideas in the 1920's* (Baton Rouge, 1954); and Edward C. Kirkland, *Dream and Thought in the Business Community, 1860–1900* (Ithaca, 1956).

Particularly useful was John H. Bunzel, "The General Ideology of American Small Business," *Political Science Quarterly*, LXX

170

(March, 1955), 87–102, from which the quotations from the National Federation of Independent Business and the Conference of American Small Business Organizations are taken.

Chapter 9. Statesman, or the Politician Transfigured

The disapproval of the politician, the distrust of party politics, and the general impression that politics is a "dirty business" are ideas that no historian of American politics has ignored. Three accounts of the development of American political parties were used here extensively; Wilfred E. Binkley, *American Political Parties: Their Natural History* (2d ed., New York, 1949) ; Edgar Eugene Robinson, *The Evolution of American Political Parties: A Sketch of Party Development* (New York, 1924) ; and Henry Jones Ford, *The Rise and Growth of Politics: A Sketch of Constitutional Development* (New York, 1898). Ford is especially good for the English background and has been closely followed for the discussion of the Whig prejudice against party. Also useful was Jesse Macy, *Political Parties in the United States, 1846–1861* (New York, 1924). For the general view of American politics that colors the discussion throughout this chapter, the author's greatest debt is to Pendleton Herring, *The Politics of Democracy: American Parties in Action* (New York, 1940). He has also followed, with appreciation, some of the insights of Richard Hofstadter in *The American Political Tradition And the Men Who Made It* (New York, 1954).

For the discussion of the changes in the political scene in the age of Jackson, the above works were supplemented by Carl R. Fish, *The Rise of the Common Man;* Dixon Ryan Fox, *The Decline of Aristocracy in the Politics of New York* (New York, 1919) ; and Arthur M. Schlesinger, Jr., *The Age of Jackson* (Boston, 1946).

For the denunciations of party spirit, the quotations are from the standard sources: Albert J. Beveridge, *The Life of John Marshall* (4 vols., Boston, 1916–1919), II, 75, 410; Edward M. Earle (ed.), *The Federalist: A Commentary on the Constitution of the United States* (New York, 1937), 53; Charles Francis Adams (ed.), *The Works of John Adams* (10 vols., Boston, 1850–1856), II, 152; Paul Leicester Ford (ed.), *Pamphlets on the Constitution of the United States, Published During Its Discussion by the People, 1787–1788* (Brooklyn, 1888), 320–21 (for Lee) ; Henry Adams, *History of the United States during the Administration of Thomas Jefferson* (2 vols., New York, 1930), I, 83 (for Fisher Ames) ; John C. Fitzpatrick (ed.), *The Writings of George Washington from the Original*

Manuscript Sources, 1745–1799 (39 vols., Washington, 1931–1944), XXV, 226–27; John Spencer Bassett (ed.), *Correspondence of Andrew Jackson* (6 vols., Washington, 1926–1933), II, 265; Stanislaus M. Hamilton (ed.), *The Writings of James Monroe* (7 vols., New York, 1898–1903), V, 342–43, 345–46; James D. Richardson (comp.), *A Compilation of the Messages and Papers of the Presidents, 1789–1897* (10 vols., Washington, 1900), II, 294 (for John Quincy Adams).

For a perceptive discussion of the need for symbolism and how it is met in America, see Ralph Gabriel, *Course of American Democratic Thought*, Chapters VIII and XXX. The best study of the cult of heroes is Wecter, *Hero in America*. See also Fishwick, *American Heroes*. For detailed treatment of the creation of the heroes individually, see William A. Bryan, *George Washington in American Literature, 1775–1865* (New York, 1952); Ward, *Andrew Jackson, Symbol for an Age*; Roy P. Basler, *The Lincoln Legend: A Study in Changing Conceptions* (Boston, 1935); Lloyd Lewis, *Myths after Lincoln* (New York, 1929); Benjamin P. Thomas, *Portrait for Posterity: Lincoln and His Biographers* (New Brunswick, 1947); and David Donald's two splendid essays (Chapters I and VIII) in his *Lincoln Reconsidered: Essays on the Civil War Era* (New York, 1956).

INDEX

Adams, John Quincy, father of, 27, 29; education of, 48; as college professor, 51; on professional soldier, 71; as politician, 104–105; as party man, 107, 109; republican simplicity of, 134, 135

Adlai Stevenson, by Noel F. Busch, best seller, 7; quoted, 56; irreverent handling of time-honored appeals in, 138

Ancestors, treatment of, in campaign biographies, 17–21; ambivalent attitude toward, 17; American Indian, 17; English, 18; Scottish, 18; German, 18; Huguenot, 18, 19; on *Mayflower,* 18, 19; seventeenth-century, 19; in Revolutionary War, 19–20; lack of southern or eastern European, 20; evolution of treatment of, 20–21; American ideals concerning, 21–25; as unimportant in a democracy, 21; American veneration of, 22; evidence of ambivalent American attitude toward, 22–24; explanations for American ambivalence toward, 24–25; change in attitude toward, 24–25

Arnold, Thurman, quoted, 101

Arvey, Jacob, connection with Stevenson, 105–106, 110

Athletics. *See* Sports

Bancroft, George, historian, as campaign biographer, 12

Bigelow, John, as campaign biographer, 6

Blaine, James G., inspirational value of life of, 10; on slavery, 13; an-

cestry of, 18, 19; father of, 26; mother of, 28; intellectual accomplishments of, 51; as schoolteacher, 51; as lawyer, 94

Boyhood, treatment of, in campaign biographies, 39–43; lack of attention to, before 1840, 39; evolution of treatment of, 40; the Lord Fauntleroy ideal, 40–41; the Tom Sawyer ideal, 41; athletics, 41–43; American ideals of, 43–47; the "cult of childhood," 43–44; in manuals for children, 44; in juvenile fiction, 44–45; evolution of interest in athletics, 45–47

Brownlow, Parson, journalist, as campaign biographer, 12

Bryan, William Jennings, as athlete, 42–43; intellectual accomplishments of, 51; as self-made man, 54, 55; as soldier, 66, 68; as farmer, 85, 86, 87; as lawyer, 95; as party man, 109; resemblance to Washington, 112; invocation of Lincoln, 113; financial condition of, 126; morality of, 133; republican simplicity of, 135

Buchanan, James, boyhood of, 40; birthplace of, 53; as self-made man, 54; as soldier, 65; as farmer, 88; as lawyer, 94; as politician, 105; republican simplicity of, 135

Busch, Noel F., journalist, as campaign biographer, 12. *See also Adlai Stevenson*

Businessman, successful, treatment of, in campaign biographies, 95–96; immediate pertinence of career as, 96–97; evolution of treatment of, 97; American ideals con-

Moskowitz, Belle, adviser to Al Smith, 6
Moskowitz, Henry, as campaign biographer, 6

Nevins, Allan, quoted, 46
Nicolay, John, on party participation in campaign biography of Lincoln, 6

Optic, Oliver, juvenile writer, as campaign biographer, 12; quoted, 53

Parents, treatment of, in campaign biographies, 26–30; father, 26–28; mother, 28–30; mother, as widow, 28–29; consistency of stereotype, 29; evolution of treatment of, 29; evolution of father, 29; evolution of mother, 29–30; American ideals of, 30–35; ideal of duty of, 30–31; fathers' duty, 31; mothers' duty, 31–33; changed role of, in urban-industrial society, 34–35; unchanging role of, in American ideal, 35
Parker, Alton B., education of, 49; as farmer, 88; wealth of, 126
Parker, George F., as campaign biographer, 5
Pierce, Franklin, distribution of biography of, 9; ancestry of, 19–20; father of, 27; boyhood of, 40, 44; as schoolteacher, 51; birthplace of, 53; as soldier, 66, 67, 69, 70; as businessman, 96; financial condition of, 126; religious toleration of, 132
Political ambition, candidates' lack of, 111–12
Political "bosses," condemnation of, in campaign biographies, 110
Political issues, in campaign biographies, 13–14
Political oratory, in campaign biographies, 14
Political parties, national organization of, 3–5; national committees of, 3–4; national chairmen of, 4–5; participation of, in prepara-

tion of campaign biographies, 6–7; distribution of campaign biographies by, 9; fear of, among founding fathers, 117–20; old Whig abhorrence of, 117; American ideals concerning, 117–20; condemnation of "blind partisanship," in campaign biographies, 106–10; candidates' loyalty to, 106–10; identity of approach of, in campaign biographies, 140
Politician, treatment of, in campaign biographies, 104–14; before 1840, 104–105; since 1840, 105–106; as amateur, 105–106; candidates' skill as, 106; "drafted" to serve, 111–12; identification of candidates with famous, 112–13; evolution of treatment of, 114; American ideals concerning, 114–17; advent of professional, 115–16; ambition of, American ideals concerning, 120; as American hero, 120–21
Polk, James K., boyhood of, 40; education of, 50; as party man, 107
Poore, Charles, on recent condition of campaign biographies, 137
Preconvention biographies, as publishing ventures, 7–8; reasons not included in study, 8

Raymond, Henry J., journalist, as campaign biographer, 12
Religion, treatment of, in campaign biographies, 130–32
Richard Nixon, by Earl Mazo, discussed, 138, 139
Rockefeller, Nelson. *See Rockefeller Family*
Rockefeller Family, by William Manchester, discussed, 138–39
Roosevelt, Franklin D., as campaign biographer, 6, 10, 110; ancestry of, 19; as athlete, 42; birthplace of, 53–54; and "self-made man" ideal, 56; and soldier substitute, 73; as farmer, 86; as party man, 110; wife of, 128

177

Roosevelt, Theodore, as athlete, 41; as soldier, 66, 67, 69, 72, 73; as party man, 108, 110; as politician, 111; as Everyman, 125; and children, 130; religious toleration of, 132; morality of, 133–34

Rush, Dr. Benjamin, quoted, 31

St. Elmo, novel by Augusta J. E. Wilson, quoted, 33

St. Nicholas, ideals of boyhood in, 45

Scott, Winfield, distribution of biography of, 9; ancestry of, 18; as professional soldier, 66, 67, 68, 71, 72; as politician, 106; morality of, 133

Self-made man ideal, treatment of, in campaign biographies, 53–56; log-cabin birth and, 53–54; moral essays on, 55; the wealthy candidate and, 56; American attachment to, 59–61; long persistence of, 59–60

Seymour, Horatio, not depicted as self-made man, 54; as farmer, 85, 86

Sigourney, Mrs. Lydia H., quoted, 32–33

Simplicity, republican, of candidates, 134–35

Smith, Alfred E., quoted, 3; as party man, 110

Soldier, professional, 69–72

Sports, treatment of, in campaign biographies, 41–43; evolution of American interest in, 45–47

Stevenson, Adlai E., ancestry of, 21; as athlete, 42; education of, 49–50; on "self-made man" ideal, 56; as businessman, 95; as politician, 105–106, 112; as party man, 110; invocation of Lincoln, 113

Sumner, William Graham, quoted, 57

Taft, William Howard, father of, 26; mother of, 29; boyhood of, 41; as athlete, 42; education of, 52; as self-made man, 55; as businessman, 95

Taylor, Zachary, ancestry of, 19; as farmer, 84; as politician, 106

Teacher, as influence on candidate, 50–51; candidates' careers as, 51

Thayer, William Makepeace, juvenile writer, as campaign biographer, 12

Tilden, Samuel J., ancestry of, 18, 19; education of, 50, 52; intellectual accomplishments of, 51; as farmer, 85; as lawyer, 94; as businessman, 96; as politician, 105; as party man, 110

Truman, Harry S., as athlete, 42; as soldier, 73, 73 n; as farmer, 85, 86, 88; as party man, 109; as politician, 111

Van Buren, Martin, ancestry of, 20; father of, 27; education of, 48; as politician, 105; morality of, 132

Wade, Ben, on distribution of Scott's campaign biography, 9

Walker, Stanley T., chosen by Dewey and Willkie as biographer, 6

Wallace, Lew, quoted, 26, 68, 93

Washburne, Elihu B., as campaign biographer, 6, 7

Washington, George, memory invoked, as soldier, 70, 72, 73; as farmer, 87, 88; as politician, 112, 113

Wecter, Dixon, quoted, 24

Wife, treatment of, in campaign biographies, 127–28; treatment of courtship of, 128–29

Willkie, Wendell, chooses campaign biographer, 6; ancestry of, 18; mother of, 30; boyhood of, 41; as schoolteacher, 51; education of, 52; as self-made man, 55; as soldier, 73; as farmer, 87; as businessman, 95; as politician, 106

Wilson, Woodrow, as man of the hour, 11; ancestry of, 20; as athlete, 42; as college professor, 51; education of, 52; as businessman, 95; as politician, 106; as party man, 109, 110; invocation of Lincoln, 113; romance of, 129

Youth's Companion, ideals of boyhood in, 45

Date Due